The Making
of a
Worship Leader

The Making of a Worship Leader

Dr. Jim Altizer

Sound & Light Publishing

THE MAKING OF A WORSHIP LEADER
First published in the year 2013
Sound & Light Publishing, Thousand Oaks, California 91360

Scripture taken from the HOLY BIBLE, NEW INTERNATIONAL VERSION.
Copyright © 1973, 1978, 1984, INTERNATIONAL BIBLE SOCIETY.
Used by permission of Zondervan Bible Publishers.

Scripture taken from the HOLY BIBLE, NEW AMERICAN STANDARD VERSION.
Copyright © 1960, 1962, 1963, 1968, 1971, 1972, 1973, 1975, 1977, The Lockman Foundation. Used by permission of Thomas Nelson Publishers.

COPYRIGHT © 2011 BY SOUND & LIGHT PUBLISHING

About the Author
Dr. Jim Altizer has a Doctorate in Worship Studies, a Masters in Music Education, and a B.M. in Trumpet Performance. He is a professor of Worship Leadership, and has served as a Minister of Worship for 22 years. Additionally, he worked as a professional trumpet player for 35 years. He now speaks at Conferences and Churches, and consults on Corporate Worship.

Edited by Morgan Franz
Cover photo by Jim Altizer

ISBN: 978-0-615-63801-0

First Edition
10 9 8 7 6 5 4 3 2 1

All Rights Reserved. No part of this book may be used or reproduced in any form or by an electronic or mechanical means including information storage and retrieval systems without written permission of the copyright owners, except by a reviewer who may quote brief passages in a review.

Dedicated to all who want to lead the way
then get out of the way.

ACKNOWLEDGMENTS

I am grateful for the memory and example of Don Fontana, who was my first example of a godly man, a gentle leader and a great musician. I was invited into ministry and encouraged in the process by Don Schmierer and Fred Jantz, both of whom found ways to guide and mold without asphyxiating me. I am also deeply grateful to the congregations of Quail Lakes Baptist Church in Stockton, California, and Cornerstone Community Church of Simi Valley, California, for their gracious acceptance of my leadership and development. Additionally, the many conferences, camps and concerts I have played have helped me to form the practical theology of ministry that is herein contained.

I am indebted to Morgan Franz for her tireless and encouraging editing of this manuscript. She was generous, excellent and challenging, and did not allow me to settle for "mindless drivel."

I gratefully acknowledge my family and friends, who make my life a celebration. My wife, Mary Kay, is the most encouraging partner a person can have. My marriage and my children (Taylor, Jeff, Nicole, Morgan, and my sons-in-law Brett and Jacob) are my magnum opus. However, I hope you like the book, too.

I
Towards A Philosophy Of Corporate Worship
10 Questions

The Nature of Worship
1. What is Worship? 13
2. Why Worship? 19

The Essentials of Christian Worship
3. What makes Christian Worship Christian? 25
4. What makes Christian Worship Worship? 29

The Nature of the Worship Gathering
5. Why Must Christians Gather to Worship? 35
6. How Do Individual, Corporate and Lifestyle Worship Differ? 38
7. What is the Content of Corporate Worship? 42

The Culture, Context and Conflict of Corporate Worship
8. How Do Culture and Context Influence Worship? 49
9. What Causes Conflict in the Church? 52
10. Where is Corporate Worship Heading? Postmodern Considerations 56

II
Towards Becoming A Worship Leader

Pastoral Requirements
11. The Pastoral Role of the Worship Leader 61
12. A Historical Summary of Corporate Worship 66
13. Service Planning 72
14. Piety—A Secret Life with Christ 77

Practical Requirements

15. Public Communication Skills 81
16. Arts Skills 85
17. Administrative Skills 87
18. Leadership Skills 93
19. A Theology of Technology (by Drew Walsh) 97
20. Getting the Job 101

III

Towards An Understanding Of Symbolic Action

An Introduction to Sacramental Theology

21. An Introduction to Sacramental Theology 106
22. Baptism in the Bible 111
23. Baptism Throughout History 116
24. The Covenant Meal and Communion in the Bible 124
25. Communion throughout History 131

IV

Towards An Understanding Of Sacred Time

Introduction to Sacred Time

26. A Theology of Time 142
27. A Summary of Christian Time-Keeping 147
28. The Cycle of Life—Resurrection 154
29. The Cycle of Light—Incarnation 162

V
APPENDICES

1. Private Devotional Patterns and Plans 167
2. Worship Ministry Participant Qualifications 171
3. Scriptural, Historical and Theological Worship Designs 172
4. Worship Administration Websites 175
5. Event-Planning "Pert" Chart 177
6. Concert Promotional Plan 179
7. Sample Concert Press Release 180
8. Job Websites & Interview Questions 181
9. Ideas, Actions & Responses for Corporate Worship 186
10. Website Resources 190
11. Microphones: Design & Application 193
12. Projection Software—Overview and Comparison 196
13. Music & Worship Budget Considerations 198
14. Ensemble Concepts for Worship Singers & Bands 200
15. Personal Monitoring Systems 202
16. Evaluating a Worship Service 204
17. Vocalist Tryouts 205
18. Practical Advice for Worship Leaders 206
19. Resources from Sound & Light Publishing 207

VI
RECOMMENDED LIST OF BOOKS

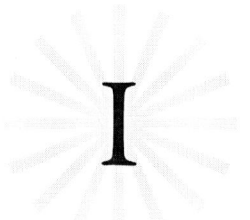

I

Towards A Philosophy Of Corporate Worship

Corporate worship is practiced in countless churches across the world each week, but rarely do we step back and ask the questions "why worship," and "why worship with others?" Asking "why" digs down to the very motivations and purposes of worship. Don Fontana, and early mentor of mine, used to say, "If you know the why, you can always figure out the how." Asking hard questions keeps a person thinking and evaluating; it helps keep the main thing the main thing. Section One of this book addresses ten questions that Worship Leaders should wrestle with. They speak to:

The Nature of Worship
What is worship, and why do it?

✠ ✠ ✠

The Essentials of Christian Worship
What makes worship Christian? What makes it worship?

✠ ✠ ✠

The Nature of the Worship Gathering
Why gather to worship?
Is corporate worship unique from individual worship?
What is the content of corporate worship?

✠ ✠ ✠

The Culture, Context and Conflict of Corporate Worship
How should Christians worship?
Why is there so much conflict about worship?
Where is corporate worship heading?

The Nature of Worship

When our first parents breathed their initial breaths and brushed the dirt from their newly created skin, they may have looked up and seen God wiping the primordial clay from His hands. They would instantly have known from whom they had come, and for whom they should live; they were created worshiping! Worship is the natural and appropriate response to the Creator God. Adam and Eve must have reveled in this natural and unhindered fellowship with their Maker, until the day that they thought they knew, or deserved, better. When they sinned, they simply traded gods and kept on worshiping.

STOP FOR A MOMENT
AND WRESTLE WITH THE FOLLOWING QUESTIONS:

How would you define "Worship"

To an atheist?
To a Professor of Theology?
To a person who is dying?

✥ ✥ ✥

Is the desire to worship

A universal human need?
A tendency?
Are there specifically Christian reasons to worship?

Chapter One

What Is Worship?

"Worship" Defined

Worship Leaders must know what worship is, so that they understand what it is not. The word "worship" comes from the Middle English word *Worthschipe*, referring to something that shows or possesses a state of worth. When the word "worship" is read in the English Bible, it is most often translated from one of two groups of Hebrew and Greek words. One definition of worship relates to acts of homage and reverence. The Hebrew word *shachah* means to prostrate, bow down, or stoop, while the Greek word *proskuneo* means to do reverence, to prostrate, or to kiss towards. A second meaning of "worship" relates primarily to labor or service. The Hebrew word *abad* means to serve or stand, and was generally used to refer to the work of the priests and Levites in their roles relating to temple worship. The Greek word *leitourgia* also refers to the service, work or ministry of worship. The English word "liturgy" comes from this understanding, and is most often defined as "the work of the people." Worship, then, refers to either reverence toward or service to God.

Although the word "worship" is often used as though it were synonymous with "praise," this is not the case. I define worship as "reflecting back to God His self-revealed worth." Worship is a response to the nature and being of God, while Praise is a response to His works. Using marriage as an analogy, "praise" would be like boasting about the great things your spouse has accomplished, while "worship" would resemble appreciating your spouse because he or she is loyal, compassionate, honest and encouraging. Praise focuses on deeds, while worship focuses on character.

When we worship, we participate in a unique cycle of communication; what theologians call the "dialogical process." Simply put, it consists of God revealing Himself to humans, and humans responding accordingly. In other words, God shows and tells what He is like, and humans respond in both praise and worship. Luther says of Christian worship "that nothing else be done in it than that our dear Lord himself talk to us through his holy word and that we, in turn, talk to him in prayer and song of praise."[1] Orthodox

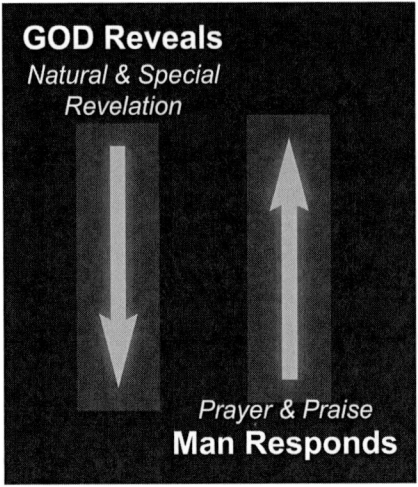

GOD Reveals
Natural & Special Revelation

Prayer & Praise
Man Responds

theologian George Florovsky states, "Christian worship is the response of men to the Divine call, to the 'mighty deeds' of God culminating in the redemptive act of Christ."[2] The numerous Scriptural examples of this revelation-response dialogue provide both a model and a Biblical precedent. The "Shamah" of Deuteronomy 6 and the Apostle Peter's sermon of Acts 2 are just two examples of this exchange. There is the intentional declaration of truth about God, and the response of God's people to that proclaimed truth. The foundational Christian principle is that God always has the first word and makes the first move towards his creation. First God reveals, and then we respond.

How does God reveal Himself to us? There are two categories of revelation: natural (general) and special (specific). Natural revelation is available to all people, at all times, in all places. It includes both creation and conscience. Special revelation is more limited, and includes Scripture, prophecy, theophany, and the incarnate Christ. Not everyone has access to special revelation, so they are more specific in nature. Whether by special or natural revelation, it is a gift that God has shown himself to Mankind. He must want to be known, even in a limited way, by those He brought into existence.

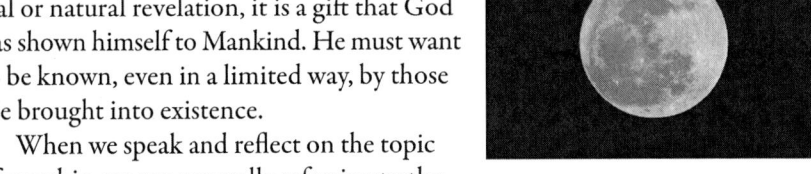

When we speak and reflect on the topic of worship, we are generally referring to the Human end of the equation; our *response* to God's attributes. A helpful picture of worship is the Moon, which has no light of its own, but simply reflects the light of the Sun back to it. Theologian A.W. Tozer described worship as "astonished reverence, breathless adoration, awesome fascination, and lofty admiration."[3] To worship, then, could be described as standing in the light and revelation of the Triune God, and reflecting his attributes, magnitude and excellence back to Him.

Avenues of Worship

There are three avenues of worship that the Christian is privileged to practice. First, the follower of Christ should develop the habit of *individual* worship.

Scripture describes a Christian as the temple of God, and says that God's very Spirit dwells in them (1 Cor. 3:16). This communion between a mortal person and an immortal God is difficult to define or describe. Various terms refer to the meeting place of creature and Creator: the "secret place" (Ps. 27:5), the "inmost place" (Ps. 51) and the "inner being" (Eph. 3:16). There seems to be an intersection of time and eternity where mortals are privileged to commune with The Divine. The Apostle Paul pens a wonderful outcome of having Christ dwell in the "inner being".

> I pray that out of his glorious riches he may strengthen you with power through his Spirit in your inner being, so that Christ may dwell in your hearts through faith. And I pray that you, being rooted and established in love, may have power, together with all the saints, to grasp how wide and long and high and deep is the love of Christ, and to know this love that surpasses knowledge—that you may be filled to the measure of all the fullness of God. (Eph. 3:16–19)

The notion that mere mortals can know, be filled with, and personally experience the Living God is unfathomable but true.

A second avenue of worship is *corporate* worship. Some question the need to join with others in corporate worship since a person is able to worship in private, but both are important and both are Biblical. The Apostle Peter addressed Christ-followers in cooperative, communal terms like "people," "priesthood" and "nation." But to what end? Peter continues, "That you may declare the praises of Him who called you out of darkness into His wonderful light" (1 Pt. 2:9). And Jesus seemed to attach special significance to the gathering with His promise, "For where two or three come together in my name, there am I with them" (Matt. 18:20). Christ does not manifest himself differently to the individual than He does to the gathered Believers, for He does not change. Rather, it is those gathered who change; "I" becomes "we."

In corporate worship, the many become one, and reflect the very nature of the Triune God: simultaneously singular and plural (more on this in Chapter 5). As they worship corporately, Christians respond to God through the presence of The Holy Spirit and through one another. This dual audience in corporate worship is reflected in Paul's writings to the Ephesians: "Speak to one another with psalms, hymns and spiritual songs. Sing and make music in your heart to the Lord, always giving thanks to God the Father for everything, in the name of our Lord Jesus Christ" (Eph. 5:19–20). In other words, we sing to God and to one another. Additionally, author Walter Brueggemann notes that corporate action not only addresses God, but also helps to construct the theological world in which we interact with Him.[4] Corporate action, then, is not merely responsive, but is also constitutive, in that it incarnates the Kingdom of God in our midst.

Finally, the Disciple of Christ engages in a *lifestyle* of worship. This means that Christ-followers demonstrate their love, and thereby their worship, through their obedience to God. Jesus said, "Whoever has my commands and obeys them, he is the one who loves me" (Jn. 14:21). This is why, when tempted by Satan to trade gods, Jesus replied, "Worship the Lord your God, and serve him only" (Matt. 4:10). The Apostle Paul undergirds the importance of obedience by urging Christians to consider the mercies they had received, and to worship by offering themselves as living sacrifices (Rom. 12:1). Scripture does not demand perfection; we all know that 'living sacrifices tend to crawl off the altar.' The daily life of a worshiper, however, is fueled by God's mercies to live a life that is pleasing to God.

"Praise" Defined

Since God's attributes are so entwined with his actions, it is sometimes difficult to distinguish his deeds from his traits. The biblical word "praise" is most often a translation of the Hebrew word *halal*, or its Greek counterpart *ainos*. Scholar Ronald Allen notes that *Halal* implies not only an imperative to boast, but also a sense of exclamation and abandonment.[5] "Someone paid my rent!" would be an example of *halal*. When *halal* is directed towards *Yah*, a shortened form of the name *YAWEH* (God's holy, unspeakable name), we arrive at the word *hallelujah*, usually translated "praise the LORD!" *Hallelujah* has become so much a part of the Christian's vocabulary that it is often not translated at all; the word itself has become an exclamation of praise. (As a side note, different spellings or pronunciations, such as "alleluia" are sometimes used, and are completely acceptable.)

I define "praise" as *active boasting in the acts of God*. Let me explain each part of this definition. Just as the ancient Hebrews could not have conceived of a God who does nothing, neither could their praise have remained static; they had to embody it (Luke 19:40). Their need to incarnate their praise is much like the difference between reading a book on swimming and actually getting wet. Praise is like jumping into the water; it is **active**. Second, "praise" is **boasting**. In the ancient world, the Israelites were faced with a whole host of gods, such as the Canaanite god Baal. In this context, "Praise" resembled the childlike boast "my Dad can beat up your Dad," as in Psalm 96:4–5: "For great is the LORD and most worthy of praise; he is to be feared above all gods. For all the gods of the nations are idols, but the LORD made the heavens."

Finally, "praise" is acknowledging the **acts of God**. If, for example, you see a turtle on a fencepost, the immediate assumption is that the turtle did not get there by itself; someone else put it there. The inherent understanding in "praise" is that God has done something that is obviously beyond our ability and cunning. As Deuteronomy 10:21 states: "He is your praise . . . who performed for you those great and awesome wonders you saw with your own eyes." The biblical word "praise," then, is a tangible recognition of God's divine interventions: *active boasting in the acts of God.*

Investigating Praise

One question regarding "praise" is "**Who** should actually do this boasting about the acts of God?" Scripture is clear that praise is expected of all servants of God, "small and great" (Rev. 19:5), and that eventually all creatures will praise him (Ps. 150:6; Rev. 5:13). A second question is "**Why** praise?" In addition to the fact that *halal* is an imperative (a command), Scripture asserts that praise is fitting for creatures, and befitting the Creator, as in Psalm 147:1: "Praise the LORD. How good it is to sing praises to our God, how pleasant and fitting to praise him!" In other words, "praise" fits; it fits us as though we were designed for that very purpose, and it fits God because He does such amazing things.

The question of "**when**" to praise has far-reaching implications. Hebrews 13:15 calls us to "continually offer to God a sacrifice of praise—the fruit of lips that confess his name." Praise is to be a continuous dialogue between God and man because of what Christ has done in His victory over sin and death. This unremitting lifestyle of praise is not meant to be burdensome, but instead is a refreshing invitation to live above the fray. The continuous offering of praise turns its practitioner into a free and joyful participant in the Kingdom of God.

Praise is even appropriate when life is difficult. Scripture does not suggest that one praise God because bad things are happening, but rather, in spite of them. Paul and Silas, for example, were "praying and singing hymns to God" while in prison, and at midnight (Acts 16:25). This type of praise is both intentional and sacrificial, and requires maturity to be offered sincerely. Further, God can be praised even in the face of tragedy. The Apostle Peter writes to the persecuted Christians, "These [sufferings] have come so that your faith . . . may be proved genuine and may result in praise, glory and honor when Jesus Christ is revealed" (1 Pt. 1:7). In the face of difficulty, praise is an amazing acknowledgement that God is both sovereign and good.

There is no required location **where** God should be praised. Psalm 113:3 poetically asserts, "From the rising of the sun to its setting, the name of the LORD is to be praised." This is in keeping with Jesus' teachings that, since God is Spirit, the location of worship is no longer relevant (John 4). Finally, one may ask, "**How**" should God be praised? Light may be shed on this question by examining other less-frequent Hebrew and Greek words that are also translated or associated with "praise." They are, in reality, various types of actions. We are to *confess* His praise (romam; yadah; exomologeo), *sing* His praise (tehillah; humneo), *play* His praise (zamar: psallo) on all available instruments (Ps. 150), and *dance* His praise (*machol*). Praise can erupt spontaneously from a grateful heart, or be the result of studied preparation and refinement. Praise can be articulated in a simple song of deliverance, like Moses', or expressed through the Arts, as with Miriam when she played, danced and sang in praise of God's deliverance (Ex. 15). It has been asserted that she may have been the very first Worship Leader as she led the children of Israel in corporate praise.

These various Hebrew and Greek words infer that "praise" can be planned and ordered, or spontaneous and clamorous. Praise is always a focused boast of what God has done, and is never about us, or our praise of God. What has God done in you that you could not do in yourself? Find some concrete ways to boast about his acts in your life, and you will know the meaning of "praise."

Conclusion

"Worship" centers on the character of God, while "Praise" celebrates the deeds of God. Both expressions are Biblical; both are necessary. "Worship" and "praise" are different components of the same relationship; Christians worship God for Who he is, and praise him for what he has done. Both Worship and Praise are fitting for all creatures in all situations at all times. They should be offered everywhere and in every way.

---

1 White, *A Brief History of Christian Worship*, 22.
2 White, *A Brief History of Christian Worship*, 23, quoting George Florovsky, "Worship and Everyday Life: An Eastern Orthodox View," Studia Liturgica 2 (December 1963), 268.
3 A. W. Tozer, *Whatever Happened to Worship?*, ed. Gerald B. Smith (Camp Hill Pennsylvania: Wing Spread Publishers, 1985), 30.
4 Walter Brueggemann, *Israel's Praise* (Philadelphia, PA; Fortress Press, 1988), 4.
5 Allen, Ronald B. *Praise! A Matter of Life and Breath*. Nashville: Thomas Nelson. 1978, 64.

Chapter Two

Why Worship?

If Worship Leaders are to plan and lead effectively, they must understand *why* Christians are to worship. At first glance, worship seems to be, to quote Marva Dawn's book title, *A Royal Waste of Time*.[1] Yet, the general existence of worship rituals in all known cultures testifies to the centrality of worship to Mankind. Evelyn Underhill states that worship, in its simplest form, is "an acknowledgment of Transcendence . . . of a Reality independent of the worshipper, which is always more or less deeply colored by mystery, and which is there first."[2] It is the human acknowledgement of this mysterious and independent reality that has produced countless customs and rituals. Ronald Byars suggests that this tendency toward ritual is actually instinctive in humans.[3] He reasons that since Man is both spirit and flesh, there appears to be an innate drive to en-flesh worship through the use of signs, symbols and ceremonies. He also notes that these elements have by nature a social quality, thereby creating ritual, which Underhill defines as "an agreed pattern of ceremonial movement, sound or verbal formula, creating a framework in which corporate religious action can take place."[4]

Why The Hebrews Worshiped

The rituals of a people group often reveal what they believe about their gods, and Hebrew ritual is particularly helpful in understanding the development of Christian worship. The lyrics for much of Hebrew worship are preserved in the biblical book of "Psalms" and give a living glimpse into some of the various motives and methods of their worship. In the Psalms we see processionals, liturgical responses, songs and prayers. Because Christianity fulfills the Jewish anticipation of both a Messiah and a new covenant, Hebrew worship provides a natural foundation for the consideration of the essentials of Christian worship. The following is a brief review of the main rationales of Hebrew worship.

Covenant Obligation

A primary theme in Jewish worship focuses on the concept of covenant, and worship was part of the Jews' covenant obligation. In fact, allegiance to the various covenants was a good indicator of the current spiritual condition of the Jewish nation. Covenant-keeping demonstrated Israel's love for, trust in and dependence (or lack thereof) on Yahweh. A covenant is a political format for maintaining relationships without the use of force.[5] There were different types of covenants, usually implemented to insure peace or trading rights between a stronger and weaker nation. The various covenants instituted by God provided a framework wherein He and his People could relate to one another. In the Suzerain/Vassal type of covenant, one party is dominant while the other is subordinate, paying homage in return for protection. Paying proper homage was, in a sense, a political obligation of the weaker party, and relates to the Jews' actions toward Yahweh.

Not only is worship expected in the covenant relationship; God also commands it. Three such commands come to mind:

> You shall love the LORD your God with all your heart and with all your soul and with all your might: (Deut. 6:5)

> You shall fear *only* the LORD your God; and you shall worship Him and swear by His name (Deut. 6:13).

> Because He is your Lord, bow down to Him (Ps. 45:11).

For the student of worship, the Hebrew covenants function as reference points for understanding how Hebrew worship evolved. The major Old Testament covenants included Noahic (Gen. 9:18–17), Abrahamic (Gen. 15:9–21; Gen. 17), Sinaitic (Ex. 19–24) and Davidic (2 Sam. 7:5–16) covenants. Each covenant served as a stepping-stone towards the unveiling of the ultimate new covenant that would be written on hearts (Jer. 31:31–34). This new covenant would restore the opportunity for full fellowship with Yahweh not experienced since the Garden of Eden. The new covenant was instituted by, and fulfilled in, Jesus Christ.

The Fitting Response

Covenant obligation was not the sole motivation for worship amongst the ancient Hebrews. When a finite creature realizes he has been created by the Infinite, he becomes keenly aware that allegiance and homage are fitting and seemly. Similarly, a People who have experienced mercy in the form of forgiveness or deliverance realize that the Giver of mercy deserves their gratitude; it is appropriate. Author C. S. Lewis likens this obligation to the sense in which a work of Art deserves and demands our attention. Lewis alleges that appreciation is the correct and expected response, and adds, "if we do not admire we shall be stupid, insensible, and great losers; we shall have missed something."[6]

In Psalm 24, the Hebrews expressed the expected response of the **Creation** to the **Creator**.

> The earth is the LORD's and everything in it,
>> the world, and all who live in it;
> For he founded it upon the seas
>> and established it upon the waters. (Ps. 24:1)

In other words, everything belongs *to* God because everything was made *by* God. It is self-evident that the creature should pay homage to the Creator, and seems ample motivation for worship.

The Hebrews also expressed the expected response of the Finite to the Infinite.

> Great is the LORD and most worthy of praise;
>> His greatness no one can fathom. (Ps. 145:3)

An attitude of humbled amazement surfaces throughout the Psalms. The Psalm writers frequently became caught up in the greatness of God, and often would list the deeds or attributes of God that best illustrate the reason for their feelings of awe. Worship in this context resembles a reflex or a spontaneous expression of the heart. It is not conjured up, but simply bubbles over.

The Hebrews expressed the appropriate response of the **Forgiven** to the **Forgiver**, as shown in these words from Psalm 103:2–3:

> Bless the LORD, O my soul, and forget not all his benefits
>> Who forgives all your sins, and heals your diseases.

With these words the Psalmist shows both his awareness of personal sin and God's willingness to forgive. The praise of the forgiven reflects the spirit of a drowning person who has been thrown a life preserver, or a parched person who has received a long drink of cool water. Deep gratitude is instantly and naturally expressed.

Finally, the Hebrews expressed the expected response of the **Delivered** to the **Deliverer**.

> The angel of the LORD encamps around those who fear Him,
>> And delivers them. (Ps. 34:7)

Deliverance was a concept the Jews understood well. The festival of Passover reenacts Israel's deliverance from Egypt, and the festival of Purim recalls Esther's courage in helping to deliver the Jews from Xerxes' death edict (Esth 9:31–32). Persecution was a fact of life for the "chosen" people, and the remembrance of God's deliverance turned their hearts toward the Deliverer.

A Central Purpose of Human Existence

Scripture also teaches that worship is a central purpose of human existence. Psalm 89 describes the practiced worshiper as one who experiences God's presence constantly.

> Blessed are those who have learned to acclaim you,
> > Who walk in the light of your presence, O Lord.
> They rejoice in your name all day long;
> > They exult in your righteousness. (Ps. 89:15–16)

The Psalter describes as "blessed" those who are continually praising God. The urge to praise seems to be programmed into creation, and it appears that Mankind is not exempt from this desire. The closing doxology of the Psalter gives particular insight into the purpose of life, commanding every breathing thing to give praise to God (Ps. 150).

Why Christians Worship

Compared to its parent Hebrew religion, Christianity is given little scriptural instruction for worship. Some attribute this to the fact that early Christians were Jewish and already knew how to worship, while others recognize Christianity as a relationship, rather than a religion, making it harder to dictate exact requirements. A. W. Tozer proposed that when God created humans in his image, he gave them the capability to appreciate and admire his attributes.[7] Still, the capacity to worship does not fully explain the Christian's rationales to worship. Christians worship both in response to God's *mercies* (Rom. 12:1), and in appreciation of his *attributes* (Rom. 11:33–36). As the Eucharistic prayers states: "It is our duty and delight to offer you thanks and praise!"[8]

Invention No. 1

Methodist Liturgist Don Saliers has observed that two crucial themes of thanksgiving and doxology have emerged from religious practice.[9] Joseph Sittler employed a musical analogy to describe Christian worship. "*Dogma* and *Doxa*—what we believe and what we pray, constitute a single music in contrapuntal form."[10] In other words, belief and response go together as naturally as melody and counter melody. Tozer, too, notices two kinds of response to God: thanksgiving for his acts, and amazement at his person. However, he notes, sadly, that most worshipers rarely get beyond gratitude.[11]

Tozer further maintained that worship is the "normal employment"[12] of human beings. By way of contrast, there has been a movement in the United States to convert the Sunday service into a primarily evangelistic gathering. Whereas, historically, Christians gathered for fellowship and worship and scattered for evangelism, some Church Growth models encourage churches to gather on Sunday for evangelism, and perhaps again for a mid-week worship event. According to Dr. Ronald Allen, however, the worship of God is the priority and ultimate end of his redemptive work.[13] Though important, Peterson agrees that evangelism is not the primary purpose of the gathering, based on 1 Corinthians 14.[14] Some may object that evangelism will somehow get lost if the Church focuses primarily on worship. Tozer would counter that "practically every great deed done in the Church of Christ all the way back to the apostle Paul was done by people blazing with the radiant worship of their God."[15] Allen also agrees that corporate worship fuels evangelism.[16] Service, including evangelism, is the natural byproduct of worship.

---

1 Marva J. Dawn, *A Royal Waste of Time* (Grand Rapids, Michigan: Eerdmans Publishing Company, 1999).
2 Evelyn Underhill. *Worship* (Guildford, Surrey, UK: Eagle, 1936, revised 1991), 3.
3 Ronald P. Byars, *Christian Worship: Glorifying and Enjoying God* (Louisville: Geneva Press, 2000), 31.
4 Underhill, *Worship*, 25.
5 Janice E. Leonard, "The Covenant Basis of Biblical Worship." In *Biblical Foundations of Christian Worship*, ed. Robert E. Webber, vol. 1, *Complete Library of Christian Worship* (Nashville: Star Song, 1994), 56.
6 Lewis, C.S. *Reflections on the Psalms* (San Diego: Harcourt Brace Jovanovich, 1958), 92.
7 Ibid., 87.
8 Don E. Saliers, *Worship As Theology* (Nashville: Abingdon Press, 1994), 76.
9 Ibid., 75.
10 Saliers, *Worship As Theology*, 40, quoting Joseph Sittler, "Dogma and Doxa," in *Worship: Good News in Action,* ed. Mandus A. Egge (Minneapolis: Augsburg Publishers, 1997), 23.
11 A. W. Tozer, *Whatever Happened to Worship?*, comp. Gerald B. Smith. Camp Hill, Pennsylvania: Wing Spread Publishers, 1985, 87.
12 Andrew Hill, *Enter His Courts With Praise: Old Testament Worship for the New Testament Church* (Grand Rapids, MI: Baker Book House, 1996), xvii.
13 Ronald B. Allen, *The Wonder of Worship*. Nashville: Thomas Nelson, 2001, 21.
14 David Peterson, *Engaging with God; A Biblical Theology of Worship* (Downers Grove, Illinois: InterVarsity Press, 1992), 195.
15 Tozer, *Whatever Happened to Worship?,* 18.
16 Allen, *Wonder of Worship*, 30.

The Essentials of Christian Worship

The New Testament does not give much direction regarding the essentials of corporate worship, and when it does, it is most often correcting an abuse. Christianity is both a relationship and a religion, and is to good news to all cultures and settings. Yet, Dr. Ronald Allen stresses, even in the face of immense cultural variation, worship must be deeply rooted in biblical truths that are unchangeable.* The underlying warning is that no matter how sincere or culturally hip worship may be, there exists a line between distinctly Christian worship, and generic genuflecting to "the big guy upstairs."

SToP FOR A MOMENT
AND WRESTLE WITH THE FOLLOWING QUESTIONS:

What makes Christian worship truly Christian?

What distinguishes it from other religions,
or from generic worship,
or worship of the run of the mill deity, force
or "big guy upstairs" kind of worship?

What elements must be present
for a service to be considered Christian?

What makes a Christian gathering worship?

What turns a Christian gathering into corporate worship?
Is attendance enough?
Is worship an action?
An attitude of the heart?
Concentration?

Chapter Three

What Makes Christian Worship Christian?

Worship Leaders must firmly grasp the essentials of what makes worship distinctively Christian. In today's synchronistic religious culture, it is crucial to acknowledge and honor God as he has revealed himself to be, rather than as we think or wish Him to be. Otherwise, we may end up worshiping worship. Worse, we might inadvertently commit idolatry by remaking God in our image. Distinctively Christian worship must be both Trinitarian and Christocentric.

Trinitarian

The Trinity is a defining Christian doctrine, duplicated by no other religion in the world. I describe the Trinity as "God living in community with Himself." The Trinitarian nature of God has great implications for why and how Christians gather, which will be expounded upon in Chapter 5. If Christians are to pay homage to this God, we must season our speech, songs and prayers with this central tenet: God is Triune. Saliers goes so far as to state "no true worship is possible without the naming of the blessed Trinity."[1] The following portion of the 5th century Athanasian Creed gives an orthodox Christian understanding of God:

> That we worship One God in Trinity, and Trinity in Unity;
> Neither confounding the Persons: nor dividing the Substance.
> For there is one Person of the Father: another of the Son: and another of the Holy Spirit.
> But the Godhead of the Father, of the Son, and of the Holy Spirit, is all one: the Glory equal, the Majesty coeternal.
> Such as the Father is: such is the Son: and such is the Holy Spirit.
> The Father uncreated: the Son uncreated: and the Holy Spirit uncreated
> The Father incomprehensible: the Son incomprehensible: and the Holy Spirit incomprehensible.
> The Father eternal: the Son eternal: and the Holy Spirit eternal.

> And yet they are not three eternals but one eternal.
> As also not three uncreated, nor three incomprehensibles, but one uncreated: and one incomprehensible.
> So, likewise, the Father is Almighty: the Son Almighty: and the Holy Spirit Almighty.
> And yet they are not three Almighties but one Almighty.
> So the Father is God: the Son is God: and the Holy Spirit is God.
> And yet they are not three Gods but one God.
> So likewise the Father is Lord: the Son Lord: and the Holy Spirit Lord.
> And yet not three Lords: but one Lord.

It is both astounding and bewildering to think that God is simultaneously singular and plural; that, in the words of Athanasius, we worship "One God in Trinity, and Trinity in Unity; neither confounding the Persons: nor dividing the Substance." How does one even begin to think about this three-in-one, one-in-three God? The Godhead has unparalleled "oneness" and "threeness" and coexistence and interaction. All descriptions defy logic; all metaphors fall painfully short. Yet, each attempt to understand it stretches our staggering amazement of Him.

A standard analogy for describing the Trinity is the egg, which has both "oneness" and "threeness" (yoke; albumen; shell). However, this analogy breaks down because the "threeness" is inaccurate: each part of the egg is different in its essence, while Hebrews 1:3 states that Jesus is the "exact representation" of God's nature. A second oft-used analogy for the Trinity is water, which has excellent "oneness" (H2O) and excellent "threeness" (in its various potential forms of solid, liquid and gas) but no coexistence (triple-point notwithstanding). Under normal circumstances, each of the forms tends to gravitate toward the other.

A third analogy of the Trinity might be a 3-wick candle. This type of candle, when lit, has "oneness" (the candle), "threeness" (flames of the same essence), and coexistence (flames burning simultaneously) but **no interaction**: no community. If the flames interact too closely, they lose their individuality and become one flame. In contrast, the baptism of Jesus (Mark 1:10–11) reveals the simultaneous presence of the entire Godhead, active and interacting.

Perhaps a better (but still incomplete) analogy is when the 3-wicked candle is blown out, causing the smoke to rise and intermingle. This could illustrate what one author called the *perichoresis*: the dance of God. The truth is that this, and all other analogies, break down. The mystery of the Trinity leaves one stupefied and undone, yet wanting to engage with this communal God, and this is done through worship.

It should be noted that the word "Trinity" is not mentioned in the Bible. That does not mean, however, that this doctrine has no warrant. It is hard to

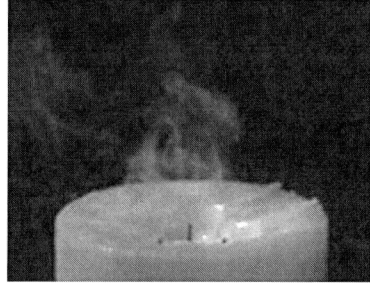

imagine God trying to make things more complicated for us. On the contrary, the Disciples and early Church Fathers embraced a Trinitarian understanding of God because they could not do otherwise; there was no other way to explain what they had witnessed and experienced. The concept of a triune God is incomprehensible, inexplicable, and indispensable. And a God Who lives in community with Himself means that *relationship* is at the very heart of the cosmos.

Christocentric

In addition to being Trinitarian, Christian worship must be Christocentric, i.e., centered on and facilitated by Jesus Christ. Regarding the centrality of Jesus Christ to Christian worship, Old Testament professor Andrew Hill submits:

> In the writings of the apostles, nothing is clearer than the fact that everything in sacred history-event, object, sacred place, theophany, cult—has been assumed into the person of the incarnate Christ. The Old Testament temple and altar with their rituals and sacrifices are replaced not by a new set of rituals and shrines, but by the self-giving of the Son of God in reconciling obedience to the will of the Father.[2]

No major Religion's view of God is completely wrong, but rather, incomplete or distorted. Only Jesus reveals God fully and clearly (Heb. 1:3). Jesus must be central in any action that purports to be Christian, especially worship.

Not only must Jesus be central, but there must also be specific belief in his regard. He must be acknowledged as Lord and God (John 20:28), resurrected and victorious (Rev. 1:17–18), as the willing and sufficient ransom for sin (1 Peter 3:18) and as the merciful forgiver of sins (Matt. 26:28). Professor and author Gerald Borchert states, "*In him* [Christ] they were facing nothing less than the mysterious divine reality itself—the subject of their worship!"[3] Christ-centered worship, then, requires the worship of Jesus as God.

Finally, Christocentric worship acknowledges that Christ himself facilitates human participation in Christian worship. In other words, Christ is our only ticket into God's presence. The writer of Hebrews (10:19) states, "we have confidence to enter the holy place by the blood of Jesus, by a new and living way which He inaugurated for us through the veil, that is, His flesh." We cannot come to God because of our righteousness. In fact, it is quite the opposite. Moses, for example, was asked to take off his shoes on God's holy ground, and Isaiah felt "ruined" when he found himself in the heavenly throne room. If you have ever accidentally walked into the wrong restroom, you may understand the feeling of being out of place. Jesus describes the concept this way:

> But when the king came in to look over the dinner guests, he saw a man there who was not dressed in wedding clothes, and he said to him, 'Friend, how did you come in here without wedding clothes?' And the man was speechless. (Matt. 22:11–12)

The feeling of being completely out of place and underdressed is a nightmare, and describes well the situation of unredeemed people in the presence of a Holy God. God has deemed human goodness to be unacceptable, but Christ has re-deemed us to be righteous, and enabled us to attend God's celebration. Peter says that Christ has "brought us to God" (1 Peter 3:18), while Isaiah declares God to have "clothed me with garments of salvation . . . wrapped me with a robe of righteousness" (Is. 61:10). The out-of-place sensation gives way to the feeling of "I am home." Our confidence to worship God is not based on our own goodness, or even on the fact that we are made in the image of God. It has been said that God looks on Christians with rose-colored glasses, stained red by the blood of Jesus. He looks into our heart, sees His Son, and declares us worthy to enter His presence. Christians are able to worship Jesus, only because of Jesus.

---

* Allen, *Wonder of Worship*, 109.
1 Saliers, *Worship As Theology*, 45.
2 Andrew E. Hill, taken from class lecture notes presented during the January 2005 session of the Institute for Worship studies, class 701.
3 Gerald L. Borchert *Responding to Mystery: A Worship Introduction to the New Testament* (Chalice Press, 2006), 78.

Chapter Four

What Makes Christian Worship Worship?

Worship Leaders may believe correct doctrine and perform the prescribed actions but still not lead worship. Psalm 4:5 states: "Offer right sacrifices and trust in the LORD." Sincerity and passion, though important, are not sufficient to ensure true worship. Tozer states, "There is worship that God will not accept, though it be directed toward him and meant to honor him."[1] Ron Allen surmises, "Only when right action is coupled with a right heart may one then sense God's pleasure. Anything less is not biblical worship."[2] I am not here challenging the notion that, in a broad sense, all of life is worship; I believe this to be true. In this chapter I am specifically probing, within the Christian community, what it is that transforms Christian activity into Christian worship. The answers to this question will be integral to both planning and evaluating corporate worship. I suggest three essential ingredients: worship must be *focused*, *wholehearted*, and must be done in *Spirit and truth*.

Focused

Perhaps you attend a Bible Study potluck, play on a Church softball team, or ride with a Christian mountain bike club. These corporate gatherings and activities are great and are uplifting, but the ingredient that turns a gathering of Believers into a worship event is a change of focus: a reprioritizing of purpose. The focal point is no longer on the food, or the game, or the ride, but is placed squarely upon God: both God in our midst and God in others. Focused worship means saying "no" to everything else, perhaps even to the things that brought the group together in the first place.

I know that multitasking is a temptation we all struggle with. It is appropriate for some situations, but not for worship. Multitasking is an enemy of worship, because worship demands all our attention. True worship is inherently opposed to multitasking. Worship will not be an item on a "to do" list, and it won't be distracted (God is, after all, a jealous God).[3] Authentic worship demands that we rebuff the desire to check our messages; refuse the grocery list; renounce stray thoughts as they arrive; repel distractions; reject all other agendas. Saliers states that authentic, worshipful response is characterized by "wholehearted attentiveness or attunement to God in and through the utterances."[4] Think of how it might feel to have dinner with someone who keeps checking his or her cell phone. Perhaps this was how Jesus felt when comparing the distracted Martha to the devoted Mary. He said that Mary, who had dropped everything to sit at his feet, had chosen well (Luke 10:42).

Wholehearted

In addition to *focus*, it is essential that Christian worship be *wholehearted*, because half-hearted love is no love at all. It is not acceptable to go through the motions; God demands and deserves wholehearted worship. Dr. Ron Allen warns that half-hearted participation in community worship leaves one under the "sad judgment of a disappointed God,"[5] referencing Jesus' words, "This people honors Me with their lips, but their heart is far from Me" (Mark 7:6). One biblical example of half-hearted worship is the Church at Laodicea, which was chastised not for incorrect doctrine, but for lukewarm devotion (Rev. 3:15–16). Additionally, the act of pretending to give wholeheartedly, while actually holding back, cost Ananias and his wife Sapphira their lives (Acts 5:1–4).

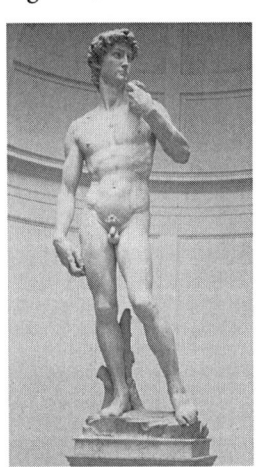

The word sincere means "without wax" and is derived from the sculpting world, wherein sculptors would cover wax with plaster to hide a mistake. True worshipers must be whole-hearted; authentic; sincere; the real deal; "without wax." When a person or a church possesses sound doctrine but halfhearted worship, they chance slipping back into a medieval enactment of piety, wherein faith took a back seat to ritual. The Roman Catholic Church has gone to great lengths to reverse a mishandling of corporate worship. The Vatican II council (1962–1965) issued the *Constitution on the Sacred Liturgy*, which calls for "full, conscious, active participation" in the rites.[6]

Half-hearted worship is not a Catholic, Protestant or Orthodox problem, but is, rather, a human problem to be strongly resisted. King David declared "I will not . . . offer a burnt offering which costs me nothing" (1 Chron. 21:24). Wholehearted worship is costly: worship that costs nothing is worth nothing. The Psalmist encourages worshipers to "bring an offering and come into His courts."[7] Both individual and corporate worshipers must offer something costly, and Worship Leaders must design and lead wholehearted worship that prioritizes the People's offering to God.

In Spirit and Truth

Jesus gave a third essential to worship by teaching that we must worship "*in spirit and truth*" (Jn. 4:24). It could be that, if rightly understood, "spirit and truth" encompass both "focused" and "wholehearted" worship. Historian James White interprets this duality as the revelation and response cycle, adding that it must be empowered by the Holy Spirit.[8] Tozer notes that true worship necessitates both (spirit and truth) because spirit without truth is helpless, while truth without spirit is "theology without a fire."[9]

Christ's comment on worship comes in the context of his discussion with a Samaritan woman (Jn. 4), and can be interpreted at least two different ways. If Jesus is responding to the woman's question of location, He may have meant that since God is spirit, the location of worship is no longer relevant. If He was responding to the woman's attempt to change the subject (from her sin), Jesus may have been referring to the need to be authentic and honest. Whether latitude or attitude, Jesus is using this "chance encounter" to speak to the woman's deepest needs.

The reader should know that theologians interpret the two words "spirit" and "truth" in a variety of ways. In an effort to further understand this central statement on worship, an examination of the two key words may be helpful. Regarding "spirit," some theologians declare Jesus to be referring to the Holy Spirit. Others read it as referring to the invisible or intangible nature of worship. Many writers have noted a Scriptural relationship between spirit and water. The water metaphor is employed, for example, as the Spirit is received at salvation (Jn. 4:14), released in living (Jn. 7:38–39), and returned to its source in worship (Eph. 5:18–20).

The word "truth" can also have several interpretations. Jesus claimed to be the truth (Jn. 14:6), but also prayed "your Word is truth" (Jn. 17:17). Paul's letter to the Colossians binds the revelation of God to the worship of gathered believers.

> Let the word of Christ richly dwell within you, with all wisdom teaching and admonishing one another with psalms and hymns and spiritual songs, singing with thankfulness in your hearts to God (Col. 3:16).

Commentator David Garland observes that "The 'word of Christ' refers to the message about Christ"[10] and that "worship is our response to what Christ has done and continues to do."[11] Garland further proposes that Scripture-centered worship will produce a more mature faith.[12] Commenting on the same verse, scholar Ralph Martin alleges that, while singing and gratitude are featured in corporate worship, hymnody must be subordinated to the ministry of teaching and exhortation.[13] The assertion that song is subordinated to the Word of God is an important principle, and its acceptance could have a major impact on the order of the Evangelical worship service.

Though Jesus' statement about Spirit and truth can be interpreted in various ways, it functions in every way as do tension and compression, bringing balance and fusion to worship. The Church must embrace this fusion of spirit and truth in worship so that they fall into neither license nor legalism. Pastor and author Steve Brown addressed these dangers in overemphasizing either spirit or truth by developing the following grid.[14]

An exclusive focus on truth and form (and the resulting dead orthodoxy) hearkens back to the Enlightenment mindset of knowledge over experience. Overemphasizing Truth leads to legalism and routine, producing policy without power. Overemphasizing Spirit can lead to license and excess, producing sensation without substance. Christ's imperative to worship in spirit and truth must drive both worshipers and Worship Leaders toward a convergence of form and freedom. These counterweights work to maintain equilibrium in worship, and result in spiritually mature worshipers (read "Disciples").

Overemphasis	Worship Focus	Result
Total Truth	Total Form	Legalism; Bondage; Dead Orthodoxy
Total Spirit	Total Freedom	Idolatry; License; Superstition
Spirit & Truth	Form & Freedom	Balance in Worship

Conclusions

As generous as it seems to consider feeling, sincerity or intensity as worship's only requirement, there are essential boundaries that define and shape Christian worship. True Christian worship must recognize God as Triune, and must center on the person and work of Jesus the Christ. Christian worship requires the full attention and costly intention of the worshiper. Finally, worship must take up residence at the crossroads of both Spirit and truth. These essentials will keep the main thing the main thing, and will determine our gatherings to be both Christian, and worship.

1   Tozer, *Whatever Happened To Worship*, 38.
2   Allen, *Wonder of Worship*, 88.
3   Ex. 20:5
4   Saliers, *Worship As Theology*, 87.
5   Allen, *Wonder of Worship*, 55.
6   *The Constitution On The Sacred Liturgy*, (Sacrosanctum Concilium, 4 December, 1963), paragraph 14; accessed May 7, 2007; www.rc.net/rcchurch/vatican2/liturgy.asc.
7   Ps. 96:8
8   White, *Introduction To Christian Worship*, 23.
9   Tozer, *Whatever Happened to Worship?*, 46.
10 David E. Garland, *Colossians and Philemon* in *NIV Application Commentary* (Grand Rapids: Zondervan, 1998), 212.
11 Ibid., 234.
12 Ibid., 236.
13 Ralph P. Martin, *Colossians: The Church's Lord and the Christian's Liberty* (Grand Rapids: Zondervan, 1972), 115.
14 Steve Brown presented this grid during his keynote address to the North American Baptist Conference in Edmonton, Alberta, Canada in July, 1987.

The Nature of the Worship Gathering

The worship service is a central and identifying occurrence in Christianity. In fact, the "gathering" is the only thing that has remained constant throughout the history of Christianity. When a person becomes a Christian, that person immediately becomes part of a community. They belong to a group that the New Testament calls "the called-out ones" (*ecclesia*).

STOP FOR A MOMENT
AND WRESTLE WITH THE FOLLOWING QUESTIONS:

Is gathering together for worship a biblical requirement? A bonus?

Are there certain Christian obligations an individual cannot achieve in solitude?

Why do you think Jesus promised to be present specifically with people who gather in His name?

Is Jesus more passionate about groups than individuals?
Is Jesus' presence different when an individual is worshiping?

Is there a specific assignment or job description for a worship service?

Is there prescribed content for a worship service, no matter the culture?

Chapter Five

Why Must Christians Gather To Worship?

Worship Leaders must understand the reasons for the worship gathering, if they are to plan worship that addresses and satisfies those reasons. As previously mentioned, a central doctrine of Christianity is that God is Triune: simultaneously singular and plural, living in community and fellowship with Himself. In the same way, the worship gathering is a theological reflection of the nature of God; it reflects the unity and community of the Trinity. Gathered Believers are individuals, but are also spiritually woven into an entity called the Body of Christ: living in community and fellowship with one another. The implications of this metaphor declare that not only *should* Believers gather, but also that they *must* gather. Four main reasons Believers must gather are to embody their corporate *identity*, to perform their corporate *vocation*, to accomplish their corporate *mandate*, and to *experience Christ in and through others*.

Identity

The first reason Christians must gather is to *embody our identity*. Though each person comes to God individually (Rev. 3:20), the Apostle Peter refers to Christians as a plurality, calling us a race, priesthood, a nation, and a people (1 Pt. 2:9–10). The Apostle Paul identifies Christians as members of the same body, and individually members of each other (Rom. 12:4–5). Unlike God, an individual can't be a community apart from gathering with others. Christians are to assemble and install themselves into the Body of Christ, just as a Stonecutter fits stones into a wall (Eph. 2:20–22). One person cannot be a body (in the group sense), but the Christian community is the Body of Christ. Further, Protestants embrace Luther's doctrine of the "Priesthood of Believers." We believe that, although one person is not a priest, gathered Christians do constitute the priesthood of God. Christians must gather in order to embody their scriptural identity.

Vocation

If Christians embody a spiritual priesthood as they gather, then what are they to do? A second reason Christians must gather is to *perform their vocation*.

Christians are a priesthood, so they should do 'priestly' things, like offer sacrifices. Peter tells Christians, "you, also, as living stones, are being built up as a spiritual house for a holy priesthood, to offer up spiritual sacrifices acceptable to God through Jesus Christ" (1 Pt. 2:5). What, then, are the spiritual sacrifices? There are four New Testament passages that specifically use sacrificial language to describe worship. The first is to offer the sacrifice of thanks and praise (Heb. 13:15). The second is the act of giving (Phil. 4:18). The third is the sacrifice of Self (Rom. 12:1–2), while the fourth is the sacrifice of service (Phil. 2:17).[1]

Mandate

A third reason Christians must gather is to *accomplish their mandate*. Followers of Christ have received marching orders, and these orders cannot be obeyed in solitude. We are commanded to gather in order to encourage one another (Heb. 10:24) and to make disciples (Matt. 28:19–20). Included in this process is evangelizing, teaching and baptizing. We simply can't accomplish this mandate in isolation.

Experience Christ

Finally, Christians gather to *experience the presence of Christ in and with others*. Jesus promised to be present when his followers gathered in his name (Matt. 18:20). When we gather for worship, we, in a very real sense, stand at the intersection of time and eternity. Walter Brueggemann calls the act of corporate worship "world-making" because it constructs a world in which the members can "viably, joyously, and obediently live."[2] World-making is done by God "through sacramental activity which God has authorized."[3] For example, at the last meal with his followers, Jesus provided a way to draw near to him through the use of both memory and hope. As Christians speak and reenact the words "as often as you eat this bread and drink the cup, you proclaim the Lord's death until He comes" (1 Cor. 11:26), there is both remembrance of His death and anticipation of his return. Both memory and hope facilitate a drawing near of God and Man (Jam. 4:8).

Concluding Thoughts

With the advancement of online communities, Church leaders are faced with new questions, as well as with new realities. Some will contend that online gatherings do not equate to real fellowship, since there is no face-to-face encounter. Others counter with the fact that, online, people are often more authentic and vulnerable than most who walk through the doors of a church. There exist a number of online Fellowships who practice Communion, while others discuss Scripture, pray together and encourage one another. Some churches have adopted a satellite model, meeting on various campuses while sharing a Speaker or Worship Leader. Wisdom, flexibility and discernment are necessary as we learn to be the Church of Jesus in a digital age.

---

1 [I am quite sure I did not discover these spiritual sacrifices, but I do not know to whom I should attribute them.]
2 Brueggemann, Walter *Israel's Praise* (Fortress Press, 1988), 6.
3 Ibid., 11.

Chapter Six

How Do Individual, Corporate and Lifestyle Worship Differ?

The mandate to gather should not lead people to infer that an individual does not or cannot experience the presence of Christ in solitude. By no means! It does, however, mean that the corporate experience is important to Jesus, and is inherently different than individual or lifestyle piety. Obviously, it is not Christ who changes from one setting to another. Rather, as has been stated earlier, it is the individual who morphs into a community. How, then, does (or should) corporate worship differ from individual devotion and from a lifestyle of worship? This is an essential question for those who plan and lead corporate worship. Four metaphors will help to explain the differences between individual, corporate and lifestyle worship. They are: a *family*, a *musician*, a *soldier*, and a *marriage*.

The Family

The individual worshiper resembles the reaction of a grateful orphan who is finally adopted. Being selected and included by the King of the universe imbues each individual with endless worth. This soul-satisfying love of God is indescribable. The notion that Christ died not just for Mankind, but also for "me" demonstrates both the extent and the magnitude of God's love, and turns each Believer into a grateful lover of God. God loves individuals (Is. 57:15), and all are privileged to both receive Him individually (Rev. 3:20), and to worship Him individually (Acts 10).

Our individual identity, however, is not all there is. This same "orphan" has also been adopted into a family with a much larger story. In corporate worship, the family reunites intermittently so that each individual can embed their personal story into God's grand story. In so doing, each participates in the celebration presently occurring in heaven (Is. 6; Rev. 4), much like joining a family reunion that is already in progress. Christians gather to retell the family's history, and to relish in their commonalities. As the anniversaries, birthdays and major events of the family are retold (church calendar), everyone gets to relive the grand story, and their particular place in it.

Worship is wider still, even extending into the world. Each member of the Body of Christ is to function, and behave, as a family ambassador. The individual's lifestyle of obedience and service shows their upbringing and respect for those whose name they carry, as well as for those who have gone before. Each member lives so as to bring honor to their People, and acts as though their actions affect more than just their own reputation. It is this lifestyle that brings glory to God.

The Musician

The individual worshiper, likewise, may be likened to a music student who sits with a master teacher, then goes off to practice and refine what they learned. Individual piety requires personal initiative and self-discipline. Practice is most often performed in solitude, and the individual Christian must develop the habit of daily, private devotion to God. Historically, this hidden devotional life seems to be the crucible in which refinement has been most often accomplished. Each Christian's calling is to "abide in Christ" (Jn. 15:4), which requires one to be crucified with Him (Gal. 2:20). The secret life of a worshiper is pursued through personal study, personal application of the Scriptures, practice of spiritual disciplines, and intimate prayer and praise.

Corporate worship resembles the music student who has joined an orchestra. Each instrumentalist lends and submits their instrument and ability to the to the conductor, to the music, and to one another, in order to produce a corporate expression. This is synergy at its best. The Apostle Peter describes this corporate calling, to "proclaim the excellencies of Him who has called you (plural) out of darkness into His marvelous light" (1 Pt. 2:9). Corporate worship, then, should be characterized by corporate actions that "offer up a sacrifice of praise to God, that is, the fruit of lips that give thanks to His name" (Heb. 13:15). When we gather, we remember, rehearse and reenact the Christ-event, just as an orchestra brings to life the musical composition of a composer.

Authenticity is proved at the strangest of times; usually when no one is looking. A lifestyle of worship, then, is akin to a Musician who performs his or her best even at an undistinguished or poorly attended concert. They live to please an audience of One, since their effort and commitment are not motivated by recognition. They give all in tribute to the Giver of the Music.

The Soldier

The New Testament describes the individual life of devotion as the life of a soldier, whose sole objective is to please the One "who enlisted him" (2 Tim. 2:4). This personal time of training and submission most resembles boot camp, where each person submits themselves to the process of becoming more than they have been thus far. Believers maintain a daily regimen of determined devotion, motivated by their love for Christ. The lover of Christ eagerly surrenders personal rights, desires, traits and mannerisms to the control of God. They lay aside self-image and self-determination in order to become like the One to whom they have tendered their lives (Lk. 9:23).

Like corporate worship, a soldier's training is often done in platoons, where group identity and allegiance are built. Soldiers live semi-communally, considering very little to be their own, and giving all to advance the group. Further, a soldier must be furloughed from time to time in order to give and receive healing, training, focus and encouragement. Likewise, Christians are commanded to gather in order to both edify others (improve the morals or knowledge of someone) and to be edified in return (Heb. 10:24). When Christians gather for worship, they should be very aware of those around them. As mentioned, gathered Believers are to sing to both God and to one another (Eph. 5:19; Col. 3:16). It is significant that most New Testament worship instruction is embedded within community instruction (Rom. 12; Eph. 5; Col. 3). Unfortunately, most churches are set-up like a classroom, and are not conducive to communal activity.

Lifestyle worship resembles the service and sacrifice of a soldier on duty (2 Tim. 2:3), and consists of personal acts of commitment and obedience. These acts are not done in order to earn God's love, but rather, in response to the love that has been received (Jn. 14:21), and as a matter of both duty and loyalty. A lifestyle of obedience demonstrates a mature love, and yields intimacy with Christ (Jn. 14:21). As someone has said, "you are who you are when no one is looking." Lifestyle worship embodies the concept of a living sacrifice, which Paul describes as our "spiritual service of worship" (Rom. 12:1).

The Spouse

Christians are the temple of God, and God's very Spirit dwells in them (1 Cor. 3:16). In this intimate and personal sense, worship parallels a honeymoon. It is a celebration of unity, identity, exclusivity, belonging, disclosure and respectful abandonment. A term

that is used for the "place" we are to hold this worshipful devotion is "the inner being" (Eph. 3:16). It is here, at the intersection of time and eternity, that mere mortals are privileged to commune with The Divine, and to actually experience and enjoy the presence of the Living, Triune God. Perhaps this is akin to joining a Trinitarian dinner party that is already in progress. In addition to experiencing "heaven on earth," a wonderful by-product of worship is penned by the Apostle Paul:

> ... that you, being rooted and established in love, may have power, together with all the saints, to grasp how wide and long and high and deep is the love of Christ, and to know this love that surpasses knowledge—that you may be filled to the measure of all the fullness of God (Eph. 3:17–19).

Ephesians 5:21–32 is the clearest passage that describes how marriage is really a picture of the manner in which Christ and his Church are to relate to one another.

What of intimacy in the corporate gathering? Jesus specifically promised to be present when we gather in His name (Matt. 18:20). "We" have reconstituted ourselves into a unique organism: his Bride, his Body, and his Church. In contrast to a honeymoon, corporate worship is analogous to a wedding ceremony or renewal of vows. Corporate worship and weddings are both celebrations of unity, identity and belonging, but the ceremony has a different type of intimacy than the honeymoon: a public intimacy. The public event utilizes symbols, vows, order and some modesty to enact the love between Man and Wife and God and His people.

People who are married understand that the wedding and honeymoon are only the beginning of a lifetime of choices. Lifestyle worship resembles how each spouse lives out their vows on a daily basis, utilizing various strategies and principles in order to make good on their vows. For example, imagine a spouse on a business trip who lives as though their partner were their constant companion. The conscious awareness that the omnipresent Christ is one's constant companion is both a joy and a refuge.

Chapter Seven

What Is The Content Of Corporate Worship?

The term "Corporate Worship" infers that Believers should do corporate things when they gather to worship. After all, one can stay home and listen to the greatest preachers, hear the most inspiring music, and read the finest prayers. Worship Leaders, then, must know and design corporate worship, and become proficient as to how to keep it fresh and meaningful. The content of corporate worship, in broad terms, should consist of corporate *revelation*, corporate *response*, and corporate *reenactment*. In specific terms, it should be comprised of corporate declaration, corporate music, corporate prayer and corporate action.[1]

Corporate Revelation

Revelation refers to the intentional presentation and declaration of Truth. Corporate revelation, then, means that gathered Believers ought to both experience and participate in the presentation of Scripture. The teaching and retelling of God's grand story should be done in many ways and forms, one of which includes the sermon. Churches should encourage and facilitate many forms of declaration if worship is to be truly corporate. Leaders must knowingly and strategically put Truth into the mouths, minds and hearts of worshipers.

The Bible models many types of corporate revelation, which can be either imitated or adapted. Psalm 29:1–2, for example, instructs worshipers to:

> Ascribe to the LORD, O sons of the mighty,
>   Ascribe to the LORD glory and strength.
> Ascribe to the LORD the glory due to His name;
>   Worship the LORD in holy array.

Worship Leaders must allow and enable the gathering, then, to fulfill these instructions. The New Testament, too, contains various examples of corporate declaration. 1 Timothy 3:16 affirms:

> By common confession, great is the mystery of godliness:
> He who was revealed in the flesh,
> Was vindicated in the Spirit,
> Seen by angels,
> Proclaimed among the nations,
> Believed on in the world,
> Taken up in glory.

Worship Leaders should also include a wide variety of declarations, both short and long. Scholar and author Ralph Martin notes that the Early Church's confessions of faith tended to be expressed in "short, simple sentences like 'Jesus is the Christ', or 'Jesus Christ is Lord', whereas their hymns were comprised of longer statements of the Person and work of Christ (Phil. 2:6–11; Col. 1:15–20)."[2] Corporate declaration also occurred through something as simple as the congregational "Amen" (1 Cor. 14:16). Truth in the form of testimony is an additional corporate act for which the Apostle Paul affirms Timothy: "you made the good confession in the presence of many witnesses" (1 Tim. 6:12). In addition to Scripture, Church history has produced various corporate confessions such as the Apostles' Creed and the Nicene Creed, which are excellent ways to involve the gathered believers in declaration. The public speaking of truth and doctrine can be both unifying and affirming.

There are a variety of ways to orchestrate the public speaking of Truth. The phrase-by-phrase repetition of small verses (a.k.a. versicles), such as Romans 12:1 or Galatians 2:20, is a great way to help people speak and identify with the Word of God. Also, one might ask people to open their Bibles to the book of Psalms and begin reading aloud the phrases of praise. The reading and explaining of Scripture (Neh. 8:1–9; 1 Tim. 4:13; Acts 20:7) is another way the gathered Believers declare the nature and goodness of God. When not read corporately, the gathered Believers must actively and vigilantly engage in hearing Scripture, listening for the overtones of God in his spoken Word.

Symbolically (and historically), corporate revelation has also taken place through both Baptism and Communion. In these acts, God's story of atonement and redemption are retold. Also, many Churches have discovered and utilized the Arts as a delivery system for Truth, using mediums such as dance and visual art to express Biblical principles. Additionally, incorporating the many symbols, calendar and traditions that Christian history has provided helps to transform the corporate gathering from a concert or lecture to a truly shared expression of Scripture and Truth.

Corporate Response

Once again it must be reiterated that Believers should do corporate things at corporate worship. Yet this is often not the case. In contemporary church gatherings, evangelical corporate worship is frequently designed to be an individual experience in a crowded room. In contrast, as has been discussed, corporate worship is distinct from individual and lifestyle worship; it has different purposes and requirements.

Music

Music is an amazing gift of God. Theologian Stanley Grenz writes that music is effectual in that it can incorporate both the cognitive and the non-cognitive aspects of life, by giving voice to "what cannot be said through words alone."[3] There are few other activities that involve body, soul, mind and emotion. Harold Best speaks of the usefulness[4] in church music, rather than style or variety. Accordingly, Donald Hustad suggests the term "functional Church Music," which he defines as music that serves both a vertical purpose (glorifying God) and a horizontal purpose (edification).[5] Quality in Church music is a difficult thing to measure, in light of the function it serves within the corporate setting. In this regard, James White warns that the music repertoire of a church must be in accordance with the congregation's culture and context, or the choosing can become elitist.[6]

References to music are scattered throughout the New Testament record (Matt. 26:30; 1 Cor. 14:26; Eph. 5:19; Col. 3:16), and generally continued many Old Testament worship practices (Ex. 15:1–18). The New Testament use of music generally employed creedal material or Scripture for its lyrics. Today, contemporary worship songs more closely resemble individual prayers, and tend to function as such, rather than theology set to music. It is important for Worship Leaders to note the tone and function of corporate music, so that it can be placed and utilized appropriately. The choosing and placement of music will be discussed in a later chapter.

Music is not worship, but is merely a tool of worship. It is, however, difficult to maintain this perspective in our musically addicted society, wherein many define themselves according to their preferred musical style. Style is a secondary issue; it does not deserve equal consideration with more central discussions of worship philosophy and theology. Many have been taught, albeit by osmosis, that worship means to stand and sing, and that each Church owes it to their people to satisfy their limited and age-identifying musical expectations. When these expectations are not met, many end-up disappointed and detached from the Body of Christ. Alternately, Churches may feel saddled with the weekly task of reenacting a Christian Rock concert in order to attract these whom they misguided in the first place. Churches may effectively alienate factions of their own Body who do not relate to a particular style of music.

Music is an incredibly effective tool for corporate response. As people sing, they enter into an alternate time (that of the song) in which mind, soul, and emotion intertwine. Sung Truth is digested holistically, not just intellectually. When Truth is artistically joined to melody, both become energized and effective. Music seems to function as a vehicle that delivers Truth to the heart. At the same time, it provides an appropriate avenue of response to that Truth by combining both mind and emotion in praise to God. Music functions like a dinner table at which both Spirit and Truth dine easily together.

A word of caution to Worship Leaders: Music, in the hands of a skilled leader, can be employed as a tool of manipulation, rather than for glorifying God. Don Hustad is convinced that church music falls short of its high purpose when *ethos* is its principal intent, or when, "for persuasion purposes, it resorts to excessive invitation to manipulation."[7] Manipulation of tempo, well-placed key changes, groove, a flowing playlist, and repetition are musical tools that are sometimes employed to get people to "feel it," or to "enter in." This feeling may or may not arise from the Spirit of God, necessitating discernment on the parts of both the worshiper and the Worship Leader.

Prayer and Meditation

Historically, public prayer was employed to rehearse God's attributes and actions before the congregation. Biblically, prayers of intercession (1 Thess. 5:25; 1 Tim. 2:1–4), confession (Lk. 11:4), praise and adoration (Matt. 6:9), supplication and thanksgiving (Phil. 4:6) are all appropriate modes of addressing God. Corporate prayer, however, can be a somewhat messy corporate action, and many churches avoid the difficulties in a variety of ways, including having one person pray (while others hopefully pray along) or by using prepared or memorized prayers. It should be noted that much of the language in contemporary worship songs, as noted above, functions as prayer. Though the language is not usually corporate, the group singing of this repertoire does resemble many aspects of corporate prayer.

The employment of litanies, such as Psalm 136, is another excellent way to involve the gathered worshipers, and is used in many liturgical services. Also, the corporate employment of silence and lamentation are two biblical but sometimes underutilized instruments of corporate prayer. The plethora of lamentation in Scripture bears witness to its importance (two-thirds of the

Psalms are laments). Saliers underscores the use of lamentation by warning that praise and thanksgiving become shallow in the absence of rage over suffering and injustice. His warning has great bearing on the design of corporate worship. Without the inclusion of lament, the life and worship of the Church will bear little resemblance to real life, and may possibly be interpreted as mere hype to outsiders.

Scriptural admonitions to use meditation are also abundant, as in Joshua 1:8. In graduate school my roommate was a geologist, evidenced by the constant sound of the rock-tumbler in our closet. The memory of that rock-tumbler has become to me a symbol of **meditation**: the slow and constant turning-over of a thought or idea. Additionally, James White champions the use of silence, but warns that its best use is dependant upon discipline. He suggests that silence comes to be fully corporate by being directed in such a way that all worshipers focus together "in confessing sin, reflecting on a lesson just read, or offering intercession." In this way, he says meditation can be intensely communal. The aspiring Worship Leader will need to give much effort to ensure that corporate prayer, including silence, is both authentic and truly corporate.

Corporate Reenactment

Symbolic Acts help to anchor the worship event between the "already" and the "not yet," and characterize the Christian gathering as a community of both memory and hope. Grenz believed one purpose of the Christian gathering was to "commemorate the foundational events of our spiritual existence, at the center of which is the action of God in Christ delivering humankind from the bondage of sin." Corporate worship, then, uses liturgical devices and activities to both remember (I Cor. 11:25) and anticipate (I Cor. 11:26), thus keeping God's story in the forefront of the believer's experience.

Liturgical activity, says Brueggemann, is an act of embracing an alternative future; an alternative world.[8] Two words are central to implementing corporate reenactment: *anamnesis* and *prolepsis*. *Anamnesis* literally means the drawing near of memory. It is not a mental process, but rather, a ritual process, through which the liturgical observance of past events somehow brings them into our own time. It is a remembrance by doing, rather than by thinking, and allows worshipers to enter into something that has happened in the past, but which becomes effective in the moment of its retelling. *Prolepsis* literally means to take beforehand, and means that worshipers can in some sense bring the future into the present by liturgically rehearsing our hope of complete sanctification and glorification.

Both baptism and communion are liturgical reenactments that vividly portray both what God has done and what He will do. Additionally, an adherence to the Church Calendar facilitates the liturgical living out of the story of God through the cycles of light and life. Even the postures of standing, lifting hands and bowing are reenactments that correspond to resurrection, rising incense, and prostrating oneself before God. It is the inclusion of the best from both ancient and contemporary that enables us to tell, experience and reenact the whole story of God.

---

1 The congregational responses employed in this study were gleaned from Scripture (Psalms and portions in the New Testament where worship gatherings and liturgical actions can be identified) and categorized according to Grenz's book *Theology for the Community of God* (Grand Rapids, Michigan: Eerdmans Publishing Company, 1994).
2 Ralph P. Martin, *Worship In The Early Church* (Grand Rapids: Wm. B. Eerdmans Publishing Co., 1964), 53.
3 Stanley J. Grenz, *Theology for the Community of God* (Grand Rapids, Michigan: Eerdmans Publishing Company), 492.
4 Harold Best, Class MUS441 discussion on October 22, 2006, Azusa, California.
5 Donald P. Hustad, *Jubilate II: Church Music in Worship and Renewal* (Carol Stream, IL: Hope Publishing Co., 1993), 24.
6 White, *Introduction to Christian Worship*, 113.
7 Hustad, *Jubilate II*, 37.
8 Walter Brueggemann, *Israel's Praise* (Philadelphia, PA; Fortress Press, 1988), 5.

The Culture, Context and Conflict of Corporate Worship

Thus far, this book has sought fixed answers to the nature and essentials of Christian worship, as well as to the very nature of the gathering. These are the things that remain unaffected by either time or culture. It is unfortunate that disagreements about worship, commonly know as the "worship wars," have not been about worship at all, but rather, about secondary things such as style and strategy. The "warring" parties continue to ask "music" questions, to the neglect of content and purpose. This is idolatry.

STOP FOR A MOMENT
AND WRESTLE WITH THE FOLLOWING QUESTIONS:

In what ways is your church's worship affected by your culture?

What is the general style and tone of your church's worship and music?

*Have you experienced, or heard stories about,
"worship wars" in the Church?*

Are these conflicts usually about Music?
Theology?
Something else?

*If you had the authority to design your church's service
this week, how would you change it?*

Can Modern and Postmodern people worship together?

What adjustments might be required?

Chapter Eight

How Do Culture And Context Influence Worship?

Worship Leaders must be students of the culture in which they serve, because humans are cultural beings. Even if we speak more than one language, we each have a particular vernacular in which we think and feel: our heart language. We also have a particular mode of dress in which we feel most comfortable, and a particular style of music that makes us feel and want to move. Our particular culture has honed our senses and sensibilities in distinct ways. It determines our immediate impressions about family, work, government, eating and God.

Our culture is deep-seeded, sub-conscious and personal. It is the way people "orient, organize and conduct themselves cognitively, affectively and behaviorally in a given time and place."[1] A person's culture will even override the ethnic and family background of a person. Author Maynard-Reid states, "Culture is not biological or racial,"[2] i.e. it is not innate. In other words, a person of Japanese descent who is raised in Texas is culturally Texan; a person of German descent raised in Mexico is culturally Mexican. Incidentally, the missionary movements of the 19th century were, in some cases, more intent on making people European than Christian. Successful evangelistic campaigns were those that respected and adapted the people's culture wherever possible.

A Church's Culture

Like people, a local church exists in a region with particular social and economic realities. It exists during a unique season in that area's existence. Therefore, a church's worship, says author Maynard-Reid, "needs to be incarnational ... culturally specific. Otherwise it will feel imposed, foreign and irrelevant."[3] A church's culture affects a Church's approach to worship.

Style is "the way we express the content within our context" says Dr. Constance Cherry. She deduces, therefore, that "style is negotiable; content is non-negotiable."[4] She continues, "each local congregation must ask **who** and **where** they are, and then express their worship to God accordingly. A common temptation is to ask, 'Who do we wish we were?' rather that 'who are we?' Falling into this trap can lead to comparisons, and leave a congregation feeling inferior."

Culture and Worship

Though the New Testament provides limited worship instruction, we can find some presence of cultural worship and practice. Since the earliest Christians were Jews, it is impossible for we who are non-Jews to imagine the difficulties of those first Christians. They experienced the laying aside of the rite of circumcision, dietary requirements, and 3,000 years of Torah in order to follow Jesus (in place of Moses). As the Gospel spread to the Gentiles, the conflict in corporate worship increased, until finally a Jerusalem Council was held to work out some of the cultural conflicts (Acts 11, 15).

In the Gentile Church at Corinth, Paul reprimands the church's abundance of favoritism, disregard for the poor, and disorderly use of spiritual gifts in public worship. The city of Corinth's culturally inspired class orientation had come into the Church (1 Cor. 14:40). In the book of Revelation, Jesus reprimands the various Gentile churches for their tolerance of bad doctrine, as well as for their half-heartedness (Rev. 2, 3). Also noteworthy is the phrase "every nation and tribe and tongue and people" (14:6). It is apparent that culture exists, or is at least distinguishable, in heaven.

An Overview of Cultural Worship Characteristics

Author Maynard-Reids has researched and collected information on various worship styles of major People groups. In order to understand the influence of culture on worship practices, I offer this summary of his findings. The following ethnic examples are meant to illustrate, rather than stereotype, how cultural settings affect a people's approach to worship. The examples are condensed from his book *Diverse Worship*. For further investigation, please read Maynard-Reid's *Diverse Worship*.[5]

There is no monolithic "Hispanic" people group; they are as varied as their many countries and regions: Central America; Mexico; South America; Cuba; Andean; Puerto Rican; Dominican Republic. Deeply influenced by the Roman church, many Hispanics consider themselves culturally Catholic, but with local influences as well. Community, passion and celebration (Fiesta) generally describe current Hispanic-Protestant worship practices, which are planned but not necessarily rehearsed. African-American Christian worship in America reflects the twin themes of liberation and celebration. Freedom in Christ is expressed in both song and movement, and services are characterized by celebration through both music and movement. Full worship is communal, vocal and physical. Caribbean culture is a complex mix of European, African and some Asian, and is more class-conscious. Pentecostal missionaries were most successful in reaching these islands, and Caribbean worship is best described as an adventure of the Spirit. Asian worship loosely reflects the hierarchy of the family unit, but is far too diverse to comment on with any specificity. This broad sweep of worship around the world should inform and perhaps warn the aspiring Worship Leader as to the effects of culture on worship practice.

Culture vs. Content

In corporate worship, Christians should use the biblical tools and means of expression (see Chapter 7) in a culturally relevant style. Culture must serve content. In other words, a local church must first embrace the overarching theological truths, and then apply them to their local, cultural practices and settings. When culture and content collide, the Worship Leader must discern whether to re-appropriate or abandon the specific cultural expressions that contradict Scripture. The most grievous example of this is found in Exodus 32, where people resorted to familiar pagan rituals to worship Yahweh. The results were immorality and idolatry. The underlying lesson for Worship Leaders is that, no matter how sincere or relevant a church's worship may be, there exists a line between what is Biblically acceptable and what is unacceptable, and they must learn to discern the difference.

---

1 Pedrito U. Maynard-Reid, *Diverse Worship* (Dowerns Grove, IL: InterVarsity Press, 2000), 16.
2 Ibid., 17.
3 Ibid., 19.
4 Constance Cherry, spoken in a lecture given at the Robert E. Webber Institute of Worship Studies, class 702 in Orange Park, FL, July 2005.
5 Pedrito U. Maynard-Reid, *Diverse Worship: African-American, Caribbean and Hispanic Perspectives* (Downers Grove, IL: InterVarsity Press, 2000).

Chapter Nine

What Causes Conflict In The Church?

One of the most embarrassing indictments of the local Church in America is its inability to stay unified. Conflict is normal, but when a congregation splits, the ramifications are staggering. A further sadness ensues from the fact that churches often split over non-essential theological differences, rather than core beliefs and convictions. Why is it that Church can seem to be the hardest thing about being a Christian? Worship Leaders are often a natural target of anger and mistrust, and must understand the many reasons conflict may occur. In addition to the human element, various causes of conflict include confusing unity with homogeneity, confusion over the purpose of the gathering, disagreement of the role of music, and a shifting culture.

Confusing Unity with Sameness

Conflict is generated when a Church confuses unity with sameness. Strategically, both Youth groups and Evangelistic events have an easier task than the local Church. They must simply use the right kind of bait for the kind of "fish" they are trying to "catch." The target group dictates music, dress and style choices for the particular ministry event. Churches, however, have a more difficult job in service design. The reason for this difficulty is the varied make up of the local Church. The Apostle Paul described the Body of Christ not in a homogenous way, but as being composed of old and young (Titus 2:2–6); rich and poor (1 Cor. 11:21–22); of varied giftedness (1 Cor. 12:4); mixed in race, gender and status (Gal. 3:28; 1 Cor. 12:13). It is tempting to simplify things by narrowing or targeting the population of your Church, but Paul makes the case that homogeneity (sameness) actually cripples the Body of Christ (1 Cor. 12:19). Unity, on the other hand, verifies both the Truth and love of God. Unity within diversity is the way of Christ. Consequently, when outsiders see the proverbial ballerina, punked-out teenager, brain-surgeon and custodian all worshiping together, they are convinced of the real Jesus, and of his love for people (Jn. 17:23). They know something supernatural is going on.

Purpose of the Gathering

A second cause of conflict is a basic confusion among congregants about the primary purpose of the corporate gathering; whether they gather primarily for worship or for evangelism. Both are essential, and neither is mutually exclusive; it is a matter of emphasis. Historically, Christians *gathered* for worship and *scattered* for evangelism. Additionally, the primary purpose for gathering on Sunday was to celebrate the resurrection. Throughout history, corporate worship's 'target population' was the gathered Body of Christ, and the service was designed around celebrating the *Christus Victor* (the Victorious Christ).

Some Church Growth models have altered the historical focus of corporate worship. In this model, the weekend gathering is viewed as the optimal time to reach unbelievers, and the gathering's primary purpose is reoriented toward evangelism. The target population becomes the Seeker, and the service is redesigned to attract and to gain access into their lives. Evangelistic services tend to target "felt needs," and are necessarily more presentational in nature. Corporate participation and symbolic action, such as communion, are often replaced by platform-based artistic offerings. This author is of the opinion that a service focused on the resurrected Christ is far more powerful, and more attractive, than anything Man can program or market. However, whatever your Church's focus, the Leadership must be clear and consistent regarding their primary purpose for gathering.

The Enthronement of Music

A third cause of conflict is that American culture has enthroned music. Music is a colossal issue! Not only is music emotional, but also people are emotional about their music. In modern culture, the style of music to which one listens has become a part of their identity and association. When people say, "I know what I like," it usually means, "I like what I know," and most people like and identify with the music of their adolescence. Christians used to assemble according to Theology, but they now often separate according to music style. The Body of Christ, however, is more like a blended family, and I believe each member should compromise to keep the family worshiping together. To redefine the Body of Christ based on musical tastes is a dangerous thing. Music is a great tool, but a lousy god.

Regarding the music itself, being really old or really new does not make a song good. Matthew 13:52 instructs teachers to bring out of the storeroom "new treasures as well as old." Psalm 96 instructs the congregation to sing "a new song," but then immediately quotes an old song from 1 Chronicles 29. The question must be asked: when music is at the very center of our self-identity, how do we allow for diverse musical expressions? One answer is that the American Church needs to reorient itself away from music-driven worship. Because of the numerous musical genres accessible on the Internet, we will never again listen to the same kind of music. Christians must find a way to deemphasize music for the sake of unity.

How do we face transitions in music and worship in a balanced way? Here are four Scriptures useful for dealing with Worship, followed by an overarching principle. Ephesians 5:19 begins with worship and ends with community. It deals with various musical forms (psalms, hymns, spiritual songs) but is followed by a command to be continually filled with the Spirit. Colossians 3:12–17 also begins with worship and ends with community. It mentions the same musical forms, this time followed by the admonition to "clothe yourselves with compassion, kindness, humility, gentleness and patience," as well as the call to bear with and forgive one another. Philippians 2:1–11 begins with community life and ends with an early worship hymn about Christ. The community instruction calls for like-mindedness, unity, and a consideration of the needs of others, followed by the encouragement to follow Christ in the laying aside of self. Romans 12:1–21 again begins with worship and ends by describing the community as a Body, imploring Christians to be members "one of another." The overarching principle for community, including communal worship, is to "make every effort to keep the unity of the Spirit through the bond of peace" (Eph. 4:3). If you want your services to be evangelistic, keep your people together! This will prove to the world both the truth and the love of Jesus (Jn. 17:23).

Human Nature

A fourth cause of conflict is simply due to a fallen human nature. Adam's sin still haunts us because each of us continues to believe that we deserve our own way. One helpful author[1] was able to look on the positive side of dealing with problematic people in the Church. He states that difficult individuals help to make the community interesting, and reveal both the strengths and weaknesses in a Church. He also said that they help us to understand what it means to live in community, while at the same time revealing the true convictions of that community. Proverbs teaches that transformation happens through tension and conflict.[2] To most, the concept of laying down one's life for one's friend[3] is attainable. It is the laying down of the *will* that is difficult.

A Shifting Culture

A fifth cause of conflict in the Church can be attributed to the shift from modern to Postmodern thought that is influencing our global culture. The world is in the midst of monumental social and cultural upheaval. The way people process thought is actually changing, and it is a very difficult day in which to do Church. This is discussed in Chapter 10.

---

1 [These excellent thoughts were taken from a past *Christianity Today*. Unfortunately, I was unable to find either the author or the article.]
2 Proverbs 27:17
3 John 15:13

Chapter Ten

Where Is Corporate Worship Heading? Postmodern Considerations

Worship Leaders must not only understand worship, but also worshipers. Changes in communication technology have affected not only the way people live, but also the way they think. For example, the Oral tradition was the *modus operandi* for most of Mankind's history. Culture, news, wisdom and ideas were most often transferred by word-of-mouth. If someone trustworthy said it, it was taken as fact. This is the era into which the Christian Church was born. *Hearing was believing*! Believers, too, participated in a largely oral tradition as they gathered at some appointed location, had a memorial meal, and listened to letters and reports of the Apostles' exploits and the ever-expanding Kingdom of God.[1]

A colossal shift took place in the 15th century when Gutenberg turned a winepress into a printing press. This was an epic milestone because it made both the documentation and exchange of information quicker, easier, and more expansive. It also removed the teacher from the transfer of knowledge and truth, something which Socrates could not have conceived. As the world slowly shifted from an oral tradition to a print tradition, a fundamental shift occurred in how people thought and knew things. *Reading was believing*.

This era enabled ideas, including those of the Protestant Reformation, to spread quickly. It also facilitated private interpretation of the Scriptures and the development of many particular branches of Christianity, giving birth to Denominationalism. A Renaissance of Art, Literature and Philosophy, and the ensuing period of extreme Rationalism, also affected Christian worship, which came to resemble a classroom more than it did a meal.

In the 20th century, a second cultural shift occurred with the advent of television. The Print tradition gave way to a multi-media culture where thought was often accompanied, and undergirded, by image. People grew accustomed to receiving pictures with their information, and, again, it changed how people thought and knew things. It was no longer enough to hear or read about an event. *Seeing was believing!* Consequently, Churches began to augment services to show, as well  as tell, the story of God, complete with props and scenery. During this period both the Television-Church and the Tel-Evangelist were born.

Mankind is in the midst of a third epistemological shift called Postmodernism. Dr. Robert Webber did a comprehensive job of articulating the changes that have led the world, and the Church, to the present junction. In Science, says Webber, thinking has shifted from a static, mechanistic view of the world to one in which the universe is in perpetual expansion. In contrast to the extreme Rationalism of Modernism, people now entertain a guarded acceptance of Mystery. Socially, the Internet has caused people to think far more globally, seeing the world as interconnected and interactive. The Postmodern mindset is far more communal, unlike the unabashed individualism of Modernity.  Communication, too, has become more symbolic, less verbal. One needs to look only as far as phone texting and the proliferation of company logos to see this fact. Additionally, postmodernism has birthed social networks where the degree of separation between people is quickly narrowing.

The Postmodern mind also processes thought differently; in this new context, *belonging is believing!* In other words, knowledge and truth are most often processed through the filter of a person's community. Other characteristics of Postmodernism are that it harbors an innate distrust of Modernity's explanation of life, as well as the logic with which it is described. Rather, postmodernism embraces the concept of *story* as a way of both explaining life and dispensing knowledge. The Postmodern Church, too, is still defining itself, seeming to know what it is against, but not as sure what it is for. This "emerging" way of doing Church includes the full spectrum of beliefs and practices, from Reformed worship to blatant heresy. Even the term "Emerging Church" no longer represents a particular people, ideology or movement; it has effectively been discarded as a specific theological brand.

Postmodern Christians

Postmoderns do not naturally assume the Bible to be authoritative, church attendance to be constructive, or the afterlife to be an accepted fact. Postmodern Christians tend to "see the Bible as infallible but not inerrant, see some forms of church attendance as constructive (mainly liturgical), and do embrace the afterlife."[2] They consider all of life as worship, especially service to others.

Postmodern Christians do not regard the Church as a building, program, institution or 503c Corporation, but rather a network of friendships.[3]

The Postmodern tendency towards Relativism is neither new nor unique to the era, but it is worrisome. Conversely, there are some distinctively Christian traits in Postmodernism. While the Modern Church seemed obsessed with trying to explain and classify the supernatural (Rationalism), the Postmodern Church seems comfortable embracing mystery and paradox, which are at the heart of Christianity. The Modern Church has grown increasingly individualistic and narcissistic, as shown by the many song lyrics that emphasize one's personal story over God's story. Conversely, the Postmodern Church tends to emphasize and value the community, often spilling over to a concern for social and global causes. This emphasis more closely resembles the Early Church, which lived semi-communally. Finally, the Modern Church embraced the Sermon (distinct from "The Word") as the centerpiece of corporate worship, to the neglect of congregational edification, Art, Scripture, Signs and Symbols. The Postmodern worshiper does not want to come to a lecture (or a concert). They want to *do* the work of worship, rather than watch it (thus their embracing of liturgy—the work of the People).

Implications for the Church

How must the Church adapt in order to have both moderns and postmoderns worshiping together as the Body of Christ? First, the Church must begin to embrace mystery by acknowledging and espousing the things that are incomprehensible, rather than trying to define and explain them. It must celebrate the paradox and mystery that is inherent to Christianity, and learn to hold knowledge in humility, being unafraid to say: "I don't know," while looking for potential answers. Second, the Church must begin to build true community, and design communal actions as a part of corporate worship. They must treat people like worshipers, rather than a glorified audience. Third, they must incorporate symbolic communication through the Arts, Christian calendar, Communion, and corporate revelation. If the Church does not adapt, then neither evangelism nor worship will be an issue. People will find somewhere to belong where the mystery is not squeezed out of life, and where they communicate in a familiar style. The Church must begin to operate as an authentic community of faith, or it will be further marginalized.

---

1 The organization of the progression of thought is drawn from *The Millennium Matrix* by M. Rex Miller (Josey-Bass: San Francisco, 2004).
2 [Morgan Franz—in discussion of this chapter on 9/10/2010.]
3 [Rich Gregory—in discussion of this chapter on 9/20/2010.]

II

TOWARDS BECOMING A WORSHIP LEADER

Worship leading involves a synergy of skills, knowledge and heart that combine to become something much more than the individual parts. Effective Worship Leadership requires an intricate combination of knowledge, wisdom, passion and skill. One must be a practical theologian in order to plan the content of a worship service. One must also have good public communication skills so that people will be able to respond to the content, rather than to the leader. Additionally, a Worship Leader is expected, in most situations, to be a good musician, because of the importance of music in our North American Evangelical culture. Dr. Robert Webber states:

> Congregations . . . should recognize the difficulty of leading contemporary worship. One cannot simply pick up a guitar, assemble contemporary instruments, pick out the right songs, and expect it to go well. Worship leading requires certain skills, a good grasp of how to accomplish the transitions from one phase to another, an ability to make the right connecting comments between songs, a strong bond with the congregation, and a heart in tune with the Spirit.*

King David personifies a combination of heart and skill that can be adapted to the training of Worship Leaders. Psalms 78:70–72 describes David's leadership of Israel: "with integrity of heart; with skillful hands he led them." This synopsis provides a framework from which to present the skills of worship leading.

Pastoral Requirements

✠ ✠ ✠

Practical Requirements

Pastoral Requirements

The following four chapters focus on the pastoral requirements of Worship Leadership. In a survey regarding church worship, Worship Leaders, Pastors and Regional Ministers were asked to list the top five *qualifications* for leading worship in the local Church. From the following categories, see if you can predict the priority of their responses.

Arts Competencies (music; visual/media arts)

✣ ✣ ✣

Correct Theology of Corporate Worship (as defined by the respondee)

✣ ✣ ✣

Administrative Gifts (leadership & equipping/coaching/team-building)

✣ ✣ ✣

Piety/Authentic heart for God

✣ ✣ ✣

Shepherd (minister; leader; calling)
(*The actual responses are located at the end of this chapter*)

Chapter Eleven

The Pastoral Role Of The Worship Leader

The role of Worship Leader is unique in the Western Church. This pastoral role requires one to be both a Shepherd and a Theologian, and includes the mandate to lead people through expressions and experiences that will immerse them into the very being of God. In this chapter we will examine the calling, the partnership, and the priestly and pastoral roles of Worship Leadership.

Calling

A calling, also known as an appointing or anointing, is an intangible and indefinable sense that God wants a person to do a very particular thing. Phrases that describe this feeling include "I feel like I'm on fire when I do that;" "I was made for this;" and "I'm working in my sweet spot." It resembles the difference between seeing a bird walk, and seeing it fly; the first behavior is awkward, while the second is in perfect keeping with its design.

A calling cannot be achieved, but must be received.

> For every high priest taken from among men is appointed on behalf of men in things pertaining to God, in order to offer both gifts and sacrifices for sins; he can deal gently with the ignorant and misguided, since he himself also is beset with weakness; and because of it he is obligated to offer sacrifices for sins, as for the people, so also for himself. And no one takes the honor to himself, but receives it when he is called by God, even as Aaron was. (Heb. 5:1–4)

Students of Worship Leadership will fall into several categories in regards to a calling. Some will have received a deeply personal call from God to the Worship Leadership ministry. Others may have a gnawing or growing awareness that God is raising them up to serve the Body of Christ, perhaps through worship leading. Still others may be studying worship leading because they are both Christian and musicians, and this training is the logical direction for their mix of gifts and abilities. Ultimately, a calling from God is what makes a person's service satisfying. Pastoral worship leading is a wonderfully difficult work, and a sense of calling is essential to long-term service in the Body of Christ.

During the time of Jesus, a Jewish Man who felt called to ministry had to have the right aptitude. After an extensive formal education, the usual path was to choose and attach oneself to a Rabbi whom you wanted to be like. Jesus, however, reversed this process by choosing his followers, rather than the followers choosing Him. Most of his disciples were regular tradesmen who had either no interest or no ability to go further into rabbinical studies. Jesus found them in the midst of their normal, established vocations and reversed the typical route to discipleship by choosing and calling them.[1] They could have said they were unwilling, but they could not have said they were unable, because Jesus called them!

The calling of less-prominent and even reluctant individuals appears to be a pattern with God. For example, He called the stutterer Moses to be his chief spokesman to the most powerful ruler in the land.[2] Gideon was the youngest person from the least influential family, and was hiding in a wine press when God called and commissioned him to lead and to conquer.[3] God sent the unpolished Peter to the highly educated Jews, and sent the educated and eloquent Paul to the Gentile world.[4] This was also David's story. In his commentary on Psalm 78, Derek Kidner notes that it is God's "sovereignty of choice" that shines through by choosing David's lineage over the more famous Joseph and more powerful Ephraim.[5] It appears that God revels in using the most unlikely suspects, perhaps so that no human can take credit for what God has done. As the Scripture says, "He puts down one and exalts another."[6]

Together in Ministry

Ministry is often difficult; perhaps that is why Jesus sent out both the twelve[7] and the seventy[8] to minister in pairs. Author Henri Nouwen believed that ministry is, or should be, both communal and mutual.[9] In most cases, the Worship Leader is working in partnership with, and in submission to, the Sr. Pastor, who should be considered the main Worship Leader. It is imperative to work with and through the Senior Pastor; to do otherwise is both impotent and divisive. The priority and vision for corporate worship should come from the pulpit rather than the Worship Leader, and collaboration between these roles is essential. This relationship must be one of trust and mutual respect if each is to serve to his/her potential. I compare the support position of the Worship Leader to Aaron and Hur, who helped to hold up Moses' tired arms during a battle[10], or to David's mighty men, who gave David's position their "strong support".[11] The Worship Leader must never try to build his/her own power-base, and must never malign the leadership of the Church. If the Worship Leader does not fully support the Sr. Pastor, and fully embrace the theology and mission of the church, he/she cannot lead whole-heartedly. Only teamwork and unity will give people confidence in their leadership.

The Role of a Priest?

There is a "priestly" type of role that Worship Leaders must temporarily assume as they escort worshipers through the divine encounter that happens in corporate worship. Author Gary Burge depicts the role as an architect of worship, where the Worship Leader functions as a type of mediator. They are to "incarnate God to the people, and forge an atmosphere of the Divine."[12] Orthodox theologian Alexander Schmemann describes this encounter in the following way: "Our entrance into the presence of Christ is an entrance into a fourth dimension which allows us to see the ultimate reality of life. It is not an escape from the world; rather it is the arrival at a vantage point from which we can see more deeply into the reality of the world."[13] It is the role of the Holy Spirit to construct and manufacture this intersection of time and eternity; it the role of the Worship Leader to facilitate the people's actions therein.

This priestly role, however, is never exercised from a position of superiority, because everyone in the Body of Christ is equal. Leaders and followers alike are akin to clay pots, *holding* the treasure, rather than *being* the treasure.[14] The priestly role of the Worship Leader, then, is based on calling and gifting, rather than perceived spiritual accomplishment. The writer to the Hebrews states that pastors can deal gently with "the ignorant and misguided, since he himself also is beset with weakness."[15]

Selecting Leaders and Platform Participants

As stated above, God seems to delight in the calling of less-prominent and even reluctant individuals (perhaps that's why He is calling you). Does it not follow, then, that as you select leaders and partners in ministry, you will not always choose the best looking or the most talented? Church leaders must always think theologically before thinking practically. We must train ourselves to look past outward things to the heart of a person (1 Sam. 16:7). Though this author is a Conservatory trained and highly experienced musician, I still prefer a pint of passion to a pound of polish in Church music ministry.

There are a variety of issues to work through when selecting people who will minister from the platform. One such issue has to do with spiritual maturity, and even whether to use people who are not publicly declared followers of Christ. Good churches come down on both sides of this issue, and the decision must be made theologically, not musically. Related to this is the question of whether to have different requirements for choir vs. worship team, or vocalists vs. instrumentalists. Additionally, one must decide issues of attitude, lifestyle, musicianship and dress. I suggest having these expectations written down and approved by your staff and governing board. Then you can hand a copy of the Church's expectations to a person, and allow them to qualify or disqualify themselves. If they don't, you now have a document from which to dig a little deeper into their lives. Appendix 2 has a sample of one Church's requirements.

Pastoral Worship Leaders do . . .

> And He gave some *as* apostles, and some *as* prophets, and some *as* evangelists, and some *as* pastors and teachers, for the equipping of the saints for the work of service, to the building up of the body of Christ (Eph. 4:11–12).

The word "pastor" (*poimen*) actually means shepherd. Since the way of Christ is to have more concern for others than for self, there must be a stripping away of self-engendered concerns. Personal preference and radical individualism are contrary to life in the Body of Christ. Scripture is clear: a pastor's job is to equip their people.[16] This means that the worship pastor must find satisfaction by watching others be successful. He/She should not attempt to satisfy his/her own performance needs at Church, but rather, should work through others. This is difficult, as the Worship Leader is often the most well trained musician on the platform. No matter! Talents and energies should be applied to helping others minister.

Pastoral Worship Leaders must know and love their congregation; even the unlovable ones. To know your people means becoming an "expert" on their demographics, tastes, traditions, history, and culture. *Knowing* and loving the congregation will enable a pastor to survive frustration, to accept criticism, and to remain joyful while growing and maturing. *Love* enables a people to trust their leader to the point of following. To withhold your heart is to reduce the congregation to an audience on which to practice one's skills on the way to a more lucrative or prestigious position. Pastor/Shepherds must lead forward at a gentle pace that the vast majority of the Church can maintain. They should continually check on the progress of the flock, stopping periodically to encourage those who have fallen behind. Rarely, but inevitably, the tough decision must be made to leave behind some who insist on having things their own way, so that the flock can move on to "greener pastures and stiller waters."

Older people often have the most difficult time with change and newness, and a word of understanding is necessary. No generation in the history of mankind has undergone the change that our older people have gone through. Some of them have gone from horse travel to space travel; kerosene to atomic energy; *Farmer's Almanac* to the home computer. Their world has changed from rural to urban, and from agricultural to industrial, to digital. Still, they, too, are a part of the "flock," and as members of the Body of Christ, each part has value and function. To worship next to someone who has known God for sixty years is an experience that cannot be had in a specific age-group ministry.

Being a pastoral Worship Leader is sometimes difficult. The stylistic changes of music and culture are difficult for everyone to navigate. A pastoral

Worship Leader must consider all members when designing worship for the Body of Christ. Mature Worship Leaders will temper their own stylistic preference and comfort with the needs of both the community and the mission of the Church. The acceptance and appreciation of the best of many styles is appropriate and necessary in the Body of Christ. Teaching one's People on worship is one way to soften the sting of change and to prepare them for the addition of new things. This may include instructing people in the concepts of worship, mixing various styles of music, and utilizing different experiences and learning styles. Change is part of life, and is good for the Church. If a people's acceptance of change grows stale, they will only tolerate stale things.

Responses to the survey for the five qualifications for leading worship in the local Church were as follows:

1. Piety/Authentic heart for God
2. Arts Competencies (music; visual/media arts)
3. Administrative Gifts (leadership & equipping/coaching/team-building)
4. Shepherd (minister; leader; calling)
5. Correct Theology of Corporate Worship (as defined by the respondee)

For reflection: Do you find these results worrying, or do they confirm your priorities about the role of Worship Leadership? How, if at all, would you change the ranking of these various qualifications?

---

* Robert E. Webber, *Worship Old and New: A Biblical, Historical, and Practical Introduction*, rev. ed. (Grand Rapids: Zondervan Publishing, 2004), 160.
1 Jn. 15:16
2 Ex. 4:10
3 Jud. 6:11–16
4 Gal. 2:7
5 Ps. 78:67–68
6 Ps. 75:7
7 Mark 6:7
8 Luke 10:1
9 Henri J. M. Nouwen, *In the Name of Jesus* (Crossroad Publishing Co., 1989), 57.
10 Ex. 17:12
11 1 Chron. 11:10
12 Gary M. Burge, "Liturgical Worship." In George Barna, et al. *Experience God in Worship* (Loveland, Colorado: Group Publishing, 2000), 64–65.
13 Alexander Schmemann, *For The Life of the World* (St. Vladimir's Seminary press: Crestwood, New York, 1988), 27.
14 2 Cor. 4:7
15 Heb. 5:2
16 Eph. 4:12

Chapter Twelve

An Historical Summary of Corporate Worship

Worship Leaders must understand the vital and formative role that corporate worship plays in the life of the Believer. How they plan corporate worship will shape the theology of their Church. This is a huge and somewhat frightening responsibility that is to be shared with the Senior Pastor. Still, the task for the shaping of a service often falls to the Worship Leader, so one must learn to think theologically about the order of service, rather than only musically.

A starting place is to know what has been done, in order to know what might be done. Christian worship can be universally categorized according to the Regulatory Principle. Simply stated, there are two schools of thought. One says that Christian worship should be regulated by what is explicitly stated in Scripture. The other states that Christian worship is to be regulated by what is explicitly forbidden in Scripture. In other words, one side will do only what Scripture says to do, while the other is free to incorporate all things not forbidden by Scripture.

History teaches, and most theologians agree, that there should be an overarching theological framework to the corporate worship event. Author Don Saliers believes that the structure of corporate worship is best expressed through enactment.[1] Liturgy professor Gordon Lathrop agrees, adding that enactment is best conveyed in prayer around the Scriptures and the Table (Communion), suggesting that it is the Word-Table community that both glorifies God and ministers to the world.[2] Robert Webber, too, contends that corporate worship is to be a "dramatic retelling" and "dramatic reenactment" of the Christ event.[3] He emphasizes worship as participation in the Christ event, especially as celebration of Christ's victory, rather than a memorial of his death. How we structure worship conveys what we believe about God, and about ourselves. An historic review of corporate worship will provide perspective on the present design of the corporate worship event.

Early Christian Worship

The earliest Christian gatherings can be characterized as a synthesis of synagogue worship and the upper room experience. In other words, the first Jewish Christians joined familiar worship elements from the synagogue to the covenant meal instituted by Christ. This format of worship is known as Word-Table, and was practiced in the fellowships of both Jewish (Acts 2:42) and Gentile (Acts 20:7) Christians. The two centuries after the Apostles and original Christians had died is known as the Early Patristic era. The gatherings of these oft-persecuted Believers were usually held in secret. Their worship order can be summarized as follows:

1) Gather
2) Read Scripture/Apostle's memoirs
3) Instruct
4) Pray
5) Communion
6) Collection for the poor.[4]

Worship in the Late Patristic Era

In 313 A.D., after the Emperor Constantine legalized Christianity, worship became more formal. Moving into large government buildings called basilicas, Christianity accumulated a certain amount of pageantry. For example, during this Late Patristic era (4th–6th centuries), the gathering and dismissal portions of the service became more formalized, and were combined with the Word-Table structure to form what Robert Webber terms "four-fold" worship, namely:

1) Entrance
2) Word
3) Table
4) Dismissal.[5]

In both Early and Late Patristic eras, the non-baptized believers (catechumens) were dismissed after the "Word" section of the service, as they were not allowed to participate in either the kiss of peace or the Eucharist.

Worship in the Middle Ages

The general script for corporate worship during the huge span of the Middle Ages (600–1500) was actually developed during the Late Patristic era, and utilized the liturgies of both of St. Basil the Great (4th century) and the Divine Liturgy of St. John Chrysostom (5th century). Eventually, the disparity of culture, leadership and theology between Eastern (Constantinople) and Western (Rome) Christianity culminated in a formal split in 1054. Eastern Christianity (Orthodox) remains largely unchanged to this day. Eastern Orthodox worship is characterized by a sense of the Believers being drawn into heavenly worship. Western (Roman Catholic) worship is characterized by a sense of heaven coming down to us, predominately in the form of the Eucharist. Communion in the Roman Church divided into two parts: the consecration, and the meal (of which most worshipers did not often partake). During the latter Middle Ages, in both branches of Christianity, worship was almost completely sacerdotal (priest-centered), effectively sidelining the people's meaningful participation in corporate worship.

Worship During the Reformation

Western Christianity experienced a second division in 1517, known as the Protestant Reformation. One goal of this movement was to return worship to the people, and Martin Luther glimpsed the possibilities for church music to accomplish this goal. Theologically and practically, music could enable that "full participation which belongs to the priesthood of the laity."[6] He envisioned a form of worship in which virtually everything but the sermon would be sung.[7] In addition to corporate singing, Protestants participated in Communion on a monthly basis. In one sense, this was a vast increase from the yearly participation of Catholic worshipers. On the other hand, the centrality of the Sermon effectively overshadowed the sacraments, prompting the criticism of "sacramental impoverishment" from the Roman church.[8] The basic service of the Protestant Reformation consisted of:

1) Gathering
2) Proclamation
3) Communion or Thanksgiving
4) Dismissal

The Westminster Assembly

The extreme rationalism of the Enlightenment prompted Protestantism to become more cerebral. Services were oriented even more toward the sermon, and were heavily influenced by the formalized creeds of the 17th century. Worship order in this era was a reflection of the Gospel story, but was so complex as to be burdensome. The practice of "Fencing the Table" referred to the warning given to all Believers who would participate in Communion, which represented an act of contrition rather than thanksgiving. The basic worship order was as follows:

1) Adoration
2) Confession/Assurance
3) Instruction
4) Response
5) Infrequent Communion (quarterly, monthly, or once per year)

Holiness & Revivalist Movements

In contrast to Westminster, the ensuing Holiness and Revivalist movements caused Protestant worship to become more personal. The service format featured an appeal for personal and public response to the Gospel, due largely to the fiery preaching of Evangelists John Wesley and George Whitfield. This corporate re-emphasis towards the personal continued to gain momentum during the First Great Awakening (c. 1720) in both Europe and America through the notoriety of both Whitfield and Jonathan Edwards.

The Second Great Awakening (c. 1787–1860), the Camp Meetings of the early 1800's, Dwight L. Moody & the Holiness Movement (c. 1870–1926), and the renewal of mass-evangelism (1950's) characterized by Billy Graham's crusades all contributed to the formation of a new paradigm for the corporate worship event. The rousing singing at these events served to gather and prepare people to receive a conversion sermon. Unfortunately, the sermon once again became more central to the gathering than the sacraments. In this regard, Byars laments, "the sermon became more prominent, while the Lord's Supper was effectively marginalized."[9] The move away from the Word-Table format and the reversal of the revelation-response cycle (singing before sermon) influences Evangelical worship even to the present day.

The Jesus Movement and the Contemporary Church

In the late 1960's and early 1970's an era dubbed "The Jesus Movement" emerged, and was centered in the southwestern United States. The movement was heavily influenced by the anti-establishment sentiment of the Hippie movement, and produced a huge number of Christian converts who were not welcomed by most mainline denominations. The Jesus movement developed a worship style that was moderately influenced by Charismatic worship, and included strong expositional Bible teaching. This "Singing and Sermon" format was sometimes followed with a strong call to conversion or to personal application.

The two-fold worship format (singing and sermon) of the Jesus Movement resembled the aforementioned Revivalist worship that developed from the 19th century Frontier Camp Meeting tradition. Today's Free Church worship service has evolved from these two service formats, and is widely practiced today.

Observations

Several observations present themselves based on this historical summary of corporate worship. The first is that the typical design of Contemporary Worship reverses the historical and biblical cycle of revelation-response by placing corporate singing prior to the sermon. This design works well for a revival, but does not make theological sense in a service of worship. The result is that worshipers are asked to respond to God before hearing from or about God, thereby placing a huge burden on song content to function as revelation. Jesus Movement Artist and convert to Catholicism John Michael Talbot stated that Contemporary worship services are "not really churches, but just real good ministry outreaches to a thoroughly secular and consumerist culture."[10] Could it be that our current Evangelical worship services are merely the longest running revivals ever?

A second observation is that our current model of music-driven worship is designed to correspond to various stages of emotional engagement.[11] The usual proof-text for this structure comes from a supposed worship progression found in Psalm 100: "Enter His gates with thanksgiving, and His courts with praise" (verse 4). Hebrew scholar Ronald Allen, however, takes issue with this interpretation. He argues: "There are NO stages to worship, as in Psalm 100. This is parallelism, not a recipe for worship! Worship is not a higher stage than praise. Praise is not a higher stage than giving thanks."[12] While these various musical and emotional stepping-stones may be effective, they cannot be proof-texted from Psalm 100.

A third observation has to do with the true corporate-ness of the contemporary worship event. Theologically, Protestants embrace the priesthood of the believer, but in practice, many churches marginalize these same Believers except during select service elements such as singing, offering and monthly Communion. The culture's affinity for entertainment has produced congregational worship that is often platform-based. Little effort is expended to make corporate prayer truly corporate, and the use of creeds and meditations is waning.

A final observation has to do with the future of the Church, and its ability to advance into Postmodernism. The marginalization of the Table (Communion), specifically, and sacred action in general, is probably a result of the Enlightenment's effect on Christianity. Robert Webber made the astounding observation that the Enlightenment affected the Church's worship more than even the Reformation.[13] I take this to mean that the balance between the rational and the mystical has been lost! The sermon has eclipsed corporate action, the worship service has become a spectator sport, and logic has displaced symbol. Unfortunately, these Enlightenment practices present a model of worship that is not compatible with the Postmodern mindset. The Modern Church offers a style of worship based on rationalism, individualism and verbal communication, while the Postmodern culture affirms mystery, community and symbolic communication.[14] The cry of the Reformation was "reformed, and always reforming." Perhaps it is time for another paradigm shift in corporate worship.

---

1. Saliers, *Worship As Theology*, 85.
2. Lathrop, *What Are the Essentials of Christian Worship*, 22.
3. Robert E. Webber, *Worship Is A Verb* (Peabody, Massachusetts: Hendrickson Publishers, Publishers, Inc. 1998), 34, 36.
4. [Summarization taken from the Didache, "The Teaching of the Twelve Apostles," a church order dating from the late first or early second century.] (http://www.earlychristianwritings.com/text/didache-roberts.html).
5. Webber, *Experience God in Worship*, 37.
6. White, *Introduction To Christian Worship*, 121.
7. Ibid.
8. Father John H. McKenna, *A History of the Mass*, (Chicago: Liturgy Training Publications, 2001), video.
9. Byars, *Christian Worship*, 25.
10. John Michael Talbot on the Ancient-Future discussion board, October 20, 2009.
11. Judson Cornwall and John Wimber use variations on these phases of worship. For a side-by-side comparison with Webber's liturgical model, see Barry Liesch, *The New Worship: Straight Talk on Music and the Church*, (Grand Rapids: Baker Books, 1996), 74.
12. Allen, *Wonder of Worship*, 124.
13. Webber's statement was made during a classroom discussion of Class 701 at the Institute of Worship Studies, Orange Park, Florida, January term, 2005.
14. Webber, *Experience God in Worship*, 41–42.

Chapter Thirteen

Service Planning

A pastoral Worship Leader is *de facto* a practical, or practicing, theologian. In fact, the planning and leading of corporate worship involves both doing and teaching theology. Worship Leaders put words and thoughts into the mouths, hearts and minds of the People of God, so it is important to have an established theology of corporate worship that will guide the many decisions made in the process of planning a worship service. Regrettably, service planning often begins with some form of the following dialogue:

"what do you want to do this Sunday?"

"I don't know; what do you want to do?"

A more recent development is for planning to begin with a song list, rather than with a theological framework. This is akin to packing for a trip without knowing the destination. Worship Leaders and Sr. Pastors alike must think and plan theologically, rather than simply choosing songs that go well together, but that have no deliberate, purposeful direction. We must be more strategic and theological.

Jesus' parting instruction was to "go make disciples," so a starting point is to discern whether the content we plan helps contribute to His mission. Robert Webber said that, ultimately, we must judge services by their content, rather than by their style.[1] Though I would add the additional criteria of being culturally engaging, we must examine the substance of the services we plan. For example: during the greeting, are the people acknowledging Christ in others, or just making small talk? Are the corporate prayers full of truth, confession, belief and thanksgiving, or just petition? And are the prayers truly corporate? During the offering, have we designed and included opportunities for worshipers to offer their very selves, or just their money? Have we designed orderly ways for people to minister to one another, or do they just take notes? Is Communion really communal; the Eucharist really thanksgiving? Protestants take pride in the fact that they don't represent Christ still hanging on the cross, so why does the typical Communion observance feel more like a funeral than a family meal?

A Theological Plan

While it is necessary to deal with the technical pieces of the worship service, Worship Leaders will miss the big picture if they only look at service parts: the "worship-set," the "sermon," the "announcements" and the "offering." Each of these plays a part in the acting-out of corporate worship, but leaders must continually remind worshipers why they do what they do. Tie each announcement to your mission statement. Turn the offering back into an act of worship. Transform the "Meet & Greet" into an acknowledgement of Christ in others. Evaluate the entire service as though it were a complete offering to God; it is all worship; or at least it *should* be.

When planning a service, be mindful of the Revelation-Response dialogue, and have a theological plan for the entire service rather than just the music portion. There are several biblical and historical plans listed in Appendix 3, but none are specifically mandated in Scripture. The guiding principle is to be sure that the order in which you do things makes theological sense. Consider, for example, whose story will be emphasized during worship; does the service emphasize, retell or rehearse God's story of creation and resurrection, reconciliation and the coming Kingdom, or does it emphasize the People's stories? Ensure that over the course of the year you celebrate the whole story of God, not just the comfortable parts. Invite and expect your people to insert their individual stories and testimonies into God's grand story; to embed themselves in something much bigger than themselves. Don't let them leave thinking their own story to be primary. Consult with the person who will preach, and brainstorm ways to integrate and synergize the various elements (music; readings; Arts; etc.) of the service. If you work with and through a creative team, bring the service elements and information to them to help flesh out the theological direction you have chosen. As leaders, you are setting the table for the heart-exchange of your people with God, and at the same time maintaining the strategic direction of your Church.

Try to think and plan everything from the People's perspective, since it is to be corporate worship. Perhaps begin the service by reminding the people of God's invitation; calling people's hearts and minds to be attentive to God's presence; providing an attribute of God on which to meditate; listening to, and about Whom, they have come to worship. Otherwise, people have to throw some mental/emotional switch (and they may not have a switch) in order to engage in worship. With none of the attributes of God being proclaimed before singing, people have to rely on personal knowledge or song lyrics to reveal God's truths and attributes. This is not satisfactory; we must respond to God He has revealed Himself to be.

As you examine the service plan, try to discern where most of the action will be happening; on the platform or with the people. Consider whether the service is an event for presentation or participation. Decide whether the gathered Believers are a congregation or an audience. If you are gathering for corporate worship, ensure the service to be truly corporate, and truly service. Make sure people recognize their responsibility to bring their offering of worship to God, and send them out with a mission.

A Roadmaps Approach to the "Music" Set

Scripture is an excellent "roadmap" for worship in that it provides a frame of reference for various songs and actions. One type of Roadmap™ is topical worship, which uses a theme, such as the attributes of God, to unify a package of songs. A second type of Roadmap™ is expository worship. This plan simply worships through a passage of Scripture, much like a preacher would teach through the passage. Expository worship not only leads people in worship, but also teaches them how to use Scripture during their individual devotional times. Isaiah 6, for example, provides verse by verse instruction for entering the presence of God (v.1–2: His presence, v.3: His worship, v.4–5: Our unworthiness, v.6–7: His cleansing). A third type of Roadmap™ is called pathway worship, which provides the worshipers with a map or blueprint for worship. The use of acronyms like A.C.T.S. (adoration; confession; thanksgiving; supplication), and designs like the layout of the temple (outer court, inner court, holy of holies) provide Scripture-based guidance for both corporate and individual worship.

In the Roadmap™ approach, Scripture provides the frame of reference. Where tastes in worship music differ, the "Roadmap" approach brings unity by placing the focus upon the Word of God, rather than the style of music. This type of guided worship provides a frame of reference that can incorporate music and action from many generations. It also provides limitless and repeatable frames of reference for worship. Emotional responses to music and beauty are never far away from the standard of God's Word, and Spirit-filled worship is more easily discerned. Scriptural frames of reference use music to deliver the revelation of God to the worshipper and the worshipper to the presence of God, rather than relying upon style, repetition or familiarity. Finally, God's Word has God's guarantee of success: "My Word shall not return void" (Is. 55:11). For a book of 100 Roadmap™ worship plans, see the book *Roadmaps for Daily Worship* in Appendix 19.

A Grid for Choosing and Placing Songs

The old phrase "Lex orandi, lex credendi" roughly means that the law of prayer is the law of faith. It suggests that how we pray helps to form what we believe. "Lex cantandi, lex credendi" is an adaptation of this rule, suggesting that what we sing forms what we believe. As pastors, we must be strategic with not only the planning of corporate services, but also with the words and lyrics of the individual parts.

The song-texts we plant in people's hearts and minds must be worthy of such a "high rent district." The Church's song repertoire ought to be a balance of prayer, lament, thanksgiving, worship and longing, rather than a steady diet of personal love songs. People should leave the service loving and knowing more about God: being more amazed; more mystified; more convinced; more stupefied at His triune being. Leaders should be careful not to lead their people to "like" one person of the Trinity more than the others. Christians should sing of God in His fullness, and enter into the middle of His three-ness; His community.

To truly understand how to judge and place a song in worship, consider the following questions:

1. Is the song a Corporate or Individual expression?
2. In the song, Who is the Subject of worship? Object? Is the song about God, or is it about the worshiper's love for God? For example, is the emphasis of the song "Jesus, Lover of my soul" or "My soul, lover of Jesus?"
3. What is the tone of song? (Praise/Prayer/Lament)
4. Whose story does the song tell? (God's Cosmic? Our/My Personal story?)
5. What type of song is it? (Psalm/Hymn/Spiritual Song)
6. Is the song relevant to your culture and context? Does the music match/undergird the text well?
7. What is the purpose of your usage? Why do you want to put these words into your People's mouths, minds and hearts?
8. What is the best placement of this song in the service?

Closing Remarks

Evaluating a worship service is difficult, but necessary. Check to see that you have planned corporate worship, rather than individual worship in a crowded room. Investigative questions to ask should include "are the people integral to the service, or could the service progress with only platform participants?" "Will your people leave asking 'God, how did I do?' or commenting on how the performers did?" "Will they think worship is 'stand and sing for 20 minutes' or understand the entire service to be worship?" Appendix 16 offers some clear criteria for evaluating a service. For additional worship plans, look again at the previous chapter (Chapter 12), as well as at Appendix 3, and adapt to your situation. There is no one biblical plan for worship, but some are more theologically based than others.

---

1 Robert E. Webber. Lecture Notes

Chapter Fourteen

Piety—A Secret Life With Christ

Piety. noun pl. pieties--ties. devotion to religious duties and practices; a pious act, statement, belief, etc.[1]

Personal piety is indispensable to the life of the Worship Leader. Piety cannot be granted or inherited; it must be cultivated. For Worship Leaders, this means that one must be devoted to growing and maintaining an ongoing, secret relationship with God above all else: above finding the right song; above the quality of the music; and above the honing of his or her musical gifts. The continual, disciplined renewal of this secret life with Christ is priority one, and there is no shortcut or substitute.

Personal piety is an attribute that is sometimes consigned to "older" or "monkish" Christians. Paul, however, dispels these myths by exhorting young Timothy to "let no one look down on your youthfulness, but rather in speech, conduct, love, faith and purity, show yourself an example of those who believe" (1 Tim. 4:12). It is self-evident that a Worship Leader should at least qualify for the position of Elder, whether or not they are included in a particular church's governing body.

> An overseer, then, must be above reproach, the husband of one wife, temperate, prudent, respectable, hospitable, able to teach, not addicted to wine or pugnacious, but gentle, peaceable, free from the love of money. *He must be* one who manages his own household well, keeping his children under control with all dignity (for if a man does not know how to manage his own household, how will he take care of the church of God?), *and* not a new convert, so that he will not become conceited and fall into the condemnation incurred by the devil. And he must have a good reputation with those outside *the church,* so that he will not fall into reproach and the snare of the devil. (1 Tim. 3:2–7).

Holy Habits = Wholly Alive

I do not advocate discipline for discipline's sake. If there were an easier way, or a shortcut, this author would have found it. With some things, however, there is no other way. For example, I'm a really good Trumpet player; it is how I fed my family and myself for many, many years. Still, I would not dream of getting up in front of people to perform unless I had spent every day in solitude, practicing. That is the cost of playing well. In the same way, the early Church Fathers understood this principle, and have left us a legacy of holy habits, known as "Spiritual Disciplines." These self-initiated practices help to develop intimacy with God, and fall into two categories: engaging and abstaining. The engaging habits include Study, Worship, Prayer, Service and Meditation. The abstaining habits include Solitude, Silence, Fasting, Simplicity and Chastity/Celibacy. I would add to the engaging list the discipline of memorizing Scripture. A Worship Leader should commit to a lifetime of Scripture memory, so that they will speak and pray God's word naturally.

I recognize that it is not easy to be in relationship with Someone who is invisible, but employing these habits can help enflesh this relationship. Be careful not to think of piety as a burdensome necessity. This secret life with Christ is amazing! It just takes steady, daily commitment. I tell my Worship Leadership students the same thing I tell my Trumpet students: "If you can't or don't want to pay the price to advance, change your major." For help in maintaining a daily devotional time, see the ideas listed in the Appendix 1.

Humble (and proud of it!)

Humility is a natural byproduct of piety, and is a fundamental attribute of a godly leader. Humility is planted on one's knees, and ripens in the "shadow" of God. Humility reflects an appropriate perspective of God, which in turn grows a realistic perspective of one's own influence and abilities. John the Baptizer was a leader who knew how to attract a crowd, and who had disciples of his own. Yet, John's greatest legacy may have been the way in which he deferred to Christ (to the detriment of his own popularity) with the words "he must increase, but I must decrease" (John 3:30). A. W. Tozer captures both the function and attitude of humble leadership with this prayer:

> Be Thou exalted over my reputation. Make me ambitious to please Thee even if as a result I must sink into obscurity and my name be forgotten as a dream. Ride forward upon me as You rode into Jerusalem, mounted upon the donkey. Let me hear the people cry to You: "Hosanna in the highest."[2]

Authentic Daily Worshiper

Piety and humility are most organically grown through the practice of authentic, daily worship. This practice is indispensable because a Worship Leader cannot lead people to a place they themselves have not been (the presence of God) and is akin to the blind leading the blind. Both the preparation and the leading of corporate worship must be done in the power of God's

Spirit, which is bestowed in secret and most often received on one's knees. There are no acceptable substitutes for God's power: it can be faked, but not for long.

---

1 www.yourdictionary.com
2 A. W. Tozer *The Pursuit of God* (Christian Publications, Inc.: Camp Hill, PA, 1982), 108.

Practical Requirements

The following four chapters will focus on the practical skills of worship leading. A Worship Leader must have excellent presentation skills, so as to clearly and confidently lead the way without becoming a distraction. Concurrent with these skills, one must usually be an advanced musician, with practical skills in both vocal and instrumental music. The Worship Leader is also expected to have good leadership skills so that others will follow, as well as administrative skills to keep the whole thing running.

Stop for a moment
and wrestle with the following questions:

Do you consider it unspiritual to employ public-speaking skills in Church?

Does relying on the leading of the Holy Spirit
replace the need to refine a person's presentational skills?

Can leadership be learned, or is it innate?

Do people energize or drain you?
What personality traits are generally associated with Worship Leaders?
What is the difference between a Worship Leader and a lead worshiper?

Why do artist-leaders generally seem to struggle with organization?

Can creativity and organization coexist in the same person?

Chapter Fifteen

Public Communication Skills

Biblical leadership is essential to corporate worship, and to living in community with one another. A mistaken notion is to describe the role of pastoral musician as the *lead worshiper*, rather than the *Worship Leader*. A lead worshiper does not actively lead, but rather behaves as one of the congregation who just happens to be worshiping in front of others. Though the humility of this concept is good, the concept itself is neither biblical nor leadership. God works through leaders (this will be discussed more in Chapter 18). Though skills alone will not make a good Worship Leader, without good skills even the most sincere, pious and theologically sound leader will become a distraction to the worship event. The skills to which I refer are those words and gestures which direct worshipers through the various responses of corporate worship, which include singing, praying, moving and meditating.

The ancient art of oratory has roots in Aristotle's text entitled *Rhetoric*, which includes three necessary ingredients for a successful presentation: *ethos*, *pathos* and *logos*. I will borrow two of these terms to address the presentational skills necessary to the role of worship leading. *Ethos* will address the non-verbal communication skills, while *pathos* will speak to the verbal skills and style of the Worship Leader. Some may contend that these skills should flow naturally out of a humble and sincere heart, and others may bristle at the thought of addressing the more physical issues of worship leading. On the contrary, just as skill can be present without spirit and heart, so can a leader's passion be masked and hindered by a lack of skill. Developing certain public communication skills are neither an attempt to deceive nor to look good, but rather, to accurately reflect the heart of the Worship Leader. If developing one's skills can remove certain obstacles for worshipers, it is a worthy use of one's efforts.

Ethos

In the classical sense, *ethos* had to do with the perceived ethical character of the speaker (is the speaker believable?)[1] and this perception is communicated in non-verbal ways. In the typical worship setting, the leader stands on a platform of some sort, while the people sit in classroom fashion (in pews or chairs) on a level lower than the platform. This separation places the leader at what is termed "public distance," wherein one's gestures become more important and symbolic than at closer "social" or "intimate" distances.[2] This separation makes it more difficult for worshipers to see and follow, and therefore certain adjustments must be incorporated into the leading of worship.

The face, eyes and hands, for example, are key points that communicate both authenticity and sincerity. Students of Worship Leadership need to ascertain whether they are perceived as authentic and sincere, since distance distorts certain visual cues. Obviously, there is a huge difference between actually being sincere, and just looking sincere, and it is entirely possible for a sincere person to appear insincere. When these distorted cues are perceived, there may appear to be a disconnect between what is said and what is communicated physically. John Wesley calls this the "silent language" that must be "well adjusted to the subject, as well as to the passion which you desire either to express or excite."[3] Therefore, poise, facial expression, eye contact and room coverage are elements that must be considered in improving the *ethos* of an aspiring Worship Leader. The employment of videotape is invaluable in this regard, in order to objectively assess oneself.

The "close" phase of public distance is approximately twelve to twenty-five feet, and is more suited to informal gatherings. The "far" phase of public distance is twenty-five feet or more, and resembles most worship settings.[4] At this distance, postural shifts are as important as spoken directives, and both speech and movement must be in agreement with one another. A postural shift involves at least half the body, and signals the end of a section or a response.[5] Effective Worship Leaders anticipate these natural breaks as they lead people toward the appropriate and desired responses.

Gesture, social distance and posture are very cultural expressions, and communicate different meanings to different People groups. Still, gestures seem to be a universal tool (even if the meanings differ), and are often divided into two categories. *Notational* gestures are gestures that communicate, and are entwined closely with speech.[6] They are a visual, kinesthetic type of movement that serves to undergird what is being said, like stretching out your hands when saying something is "huge." *Referential* gestures have more to do with signaling than with speech. These gestures give direction and are an asset when conducting worship at the public distance. For example, well-used referential gestures can signal the congregation to stand (a lifting motion) or sit (a deliberate lowering hand motion), sing with or echo (pointing to yourself or the congregation), sing loud (as a conductor signals *forte*) or listen (cupping the ear), without saying a word. The more that can be communicated by gesture, the less verbal direction the Worship Leader will need to give, thereby lessening possible distraction.

Pathos

The term *pathos* provides a platform from which to discuss the verbal skills necessary for effective Worship Leadership. *Pathos* generally refers to the way a leader appeals to the emotions, sympathies or imagination of the worshipper. It is never acceptable to manipulate or toy with people's emotions. Rather, utilizing *pathos* effectively means personalizing the message so that others can respond.[7] Good Worship Leaders are inviting and encouraging. They facilitate, but do not dominate a service. They don't give the impression that others have to feel what they feel. *Pathos* is the synthesis of both cognitive and affective (emotional) response, where what is said and how it is said combine to form a bridge on which the listening mind and receiving heart can encounter one another. A poetic tongue is required to help the community to recognize both its jeopardy and its yearning for God.[8]

Additional Suggestions

Worshipers are usually able to discern whether a leader's words and message are in harmony with one another. Therefore, material must be mastered, so that one's passion and confidence will encourage others to follow. Stammering and meandering show a lack of preparation and respect for this priestly role, and no one wants to follow a leader who is uncertain, or worse, lost. Also, since the Worship Leader must love the people he or she is shepherding, the leader should look at the people when leading. This is contrary to the practices of many song leaders who shut their eyes while leading, either to demonstrate focus, or because they are caught-up in their own experience. Visually, leaders should not merely sweep the room, though this is preferable to staring down at notes. Rather, they should pick individuals to speak to, and complete a thought with that one person.[9] Finally, Worship Leaders should use a tone of speaking that is pastoral and inviting. Mastery of good microphone technique is necessary in this regard, and must be taught and practiced.[10] While tone is important, it must not become a tool to manipulate. It is not the responsibility of leaders to make God look good, or to verbally excite worshipers. Rather, the authentic presentation of revelation, united to confident and clear leadership, is all that is needed of a Worship Leader.

---

1 Mitman, *Worship in the Shape of Scripture*, 85.
2 Julius Fast. *Body Language* (New York, New York: Pocket Books, 1970), 26.

3 John Wesley, *Directions Concerning Pronunciation and Gesture* quoted in Brett P. Webb-Mitchell *Christly Gestures* (Grand Rapids: W.B. Eerdmans, 2002), 146.
4 Fast. *Body Language*. 25.
5 Ibid., 116.
6 Brett P. Webb-Mitchell, *Christly Gestures* (Grand Rapids, MI: Eerdmans Publishing, 2003), 103.
7 Davis, *Secrets of Dynamic Communication*, 163.
8 Brueggemann, *Israel's Praise*, 45.
9 Davis. *Secrets of Dynamic Communication*, 137.
10 Ibid., 154–155.

Chapter Sixteen

Arts Skills

Most Worship Leaders will need to run rehearsals of some kind, whether choir, orchestra, band/rhythm section or a vocal ensemble. When planning a rehearsal, don't just decide which music you will practice, but exactly what you will practice in each piece. Study your music prior to rehearsal, and anticipate the problem spots. Note: extensive vocal warm-ups are less necessary at mid-week rehearsals, since people have usually been talking all day. A memorized song or simple chorus will call people together and help them begin to focus, without the director having to say anything.

Rehearsal Skills

Your group should be playing or singing at least 70% of the time that they spend in rehearsal. People join a music group because they want to make music, so keep them at it. When you stop to fix a musical problem, be sure your correction is a musical correction. "Do it again" is a meaningless comment, as people don't know what to change, and you don't have anything to reinforce, either positively or negatively. With especially difficult passages, you should striate the section. This means to break the music down into its basic parts, and add one part at a time after the prior part has been learned. Also, if you will spend two minutes of every rehearsal teaching music reading (for your non-readers), it will pay huge dividends. The following rehearsal skill-drills were developed and taught in a Video Micro-rehearsal class developed by Dr. Lawrence McQuerry at the University of the Pacific. Specific rehearsal skills should be taught, practiced, demonstrated and evaluated through use of video and playback.

Here is a typical rehearsal drill:

1. Start the music, and listen carefully, or anticipate possible problem areas prior to the rehearsal.
2. Diagnose the problem while the music is still playing.

3. Stop clearly, at a logical place.
4. Make one single correction or suggestion; say it only once.
5. Immediately restart the piece at a logical place.
6. Follow-through/Reinforce with signals (good or bad) whether or not the problem was fixed.

Worship Team and Rhythm Section skills

Generally, worship teams have a disproportionate number of non-readers (music) and a different approach must be taken from that of music-readers. The function of each member (band and singer) can be likened to separate stones being built into a spiritual house (Eph. 2). Each piece contributes either to the melody, the harmony or the rhythm. Try starting with rhythm, then adding the harmony and finally the melody in order to give people a good feel for the role they are playing. Talk about the concept of *koinonia*, and the importance of adjusting to each other on the fly. Teach this by having one person change the style of singing or playing, and asking everyone else to adjust accordingly. Teach the instrumentalists how their playing must change between a Gospel tune, a Latin tune, a Rock tune and a Ballad. If your vocalists are not reading, have them conceive of a "flying V" much like geese fly in. The lead soprano is at the front, and sets the phrasing and style. All must fall into line. Next, have your harmonizers jump in. Always have at least one male and one female singing the melody, so that the congregation can hear the melody in their own octave. Finally, have one of your better musicians do some improvising during the phrase breaks. For more information, see Appendix 14.

Congregational music skills

Situate congregational songs in accessible keys. God created some people with high voices, and some with low voices. In order to lead everyone, I suggest not going below an "A" or above a "D" especially in the morning. Consider changing the key of a song if it will help your people participate. Good Worship Leaders are also careful about how many new songs are in a set. It's advisable to do no more than one new song per set, and in a Church setting, only one new song every second or third week. If your average person attends 2–3 times per month, you're going to have to repeat the song for a few weeks, just so that everyone gets to know it. Also, try incorporating an assortment of musical styles, and playing in an assortment of keys. This maintains aesthetic interest, it elevates the culture, it expands a congregation's musical vocabulary, and it keeps things from getting boring, or worse; predictable.

Chapter Seventeen

Administrative Skills

Artistically oriented people necessarily see life differently, and are often said to 'color outside the lines.' Certain organizational skills often elude this type of person in lieu of their tendency to be creative and spontaneous. They may secretly feel that planning ahead will take the mystery and surprise out of life, and will generally tend to be rather disorganized. Unfortunately, organization is a key requirement to leading well, as people do not want to have their time wasted. A primary pastoral admonition is to "equip the Saints to do the work of ministry" (Eph. 4:12), rather than doing the work oneself. A Worship Leader, therefore, must learn the skills of organization and planning, in order to successfully administrate ministry in the local church.

Personal Organization

Begin by having only one calendar, where you write everything.[1] You must back-up your calendar regularly. Get something online that does this automatically. Decide that every day, for the rest of your life, you will do two things before you take a bite of food: 1) meet with God; 2) check your calendar. These are absolutes! Your "Task List" or "To Do" list can be much more flexible. Try to list things that either you cannot delegate, or that fulfill your personal mission and vision.[2] Structure your day by having a set time to return emails and phone calls. Handle mail and notes only once. Regarding mail, author Hugh Ballou says to either "file it, return it with notes, pass it to the appropriate person, or discard it."[3]

Additional Staff Duties

Presumably, a local Church hires a professional because a needed task can no longer be done by a volunteer. This means that a Church staff member will necessarily do a variety of auxiliary tasks as a part of their duties, and that the ability to administrate well will be crucial. A church staff member is expected to interface with other staff members, and to perform general duties such as attend staff meetings, render pastoral care, attend denominational requirements, etc. It is a weekly, even daily effort to stay up with the other ministries of the church.

Planning—The Week

Structure your week around the constant: Sunday. An effective cycle of tasks can begin on Thursday. On this day, begin thinking and praying about the following Sunday (the one after the immediate Sunday). Pray, "How do you want your people to worship You?" Take the time to listen. Get the sermon outline, and any ideas the preaching pastor may have. Jot down ideas for congregational involvement, including songs, creeds, corporate actions, etc. Take Friday and/or Saturday off, if you are allowed to choose.

On Sunday, arrive early and have an extensive personal worship time; then execute your plan (that began a week ago Thursday) to lead people in their corporate service to God. Many pastors take Monday as their day off, but I recommend against this. You will be tired, sometimes a bit depressed, and rather uncreative on Monday, so don't give yourself, or your family, your worst day. Save office tasks that require no real vision-casting or creative thinking for that day. It is also a great day to clean up from Sunday by filing the used music, and putting things in their rightful place. Oil squeaky sanctuary doors. Note any equipment that needs repair, and schedule a fix. Check on any auxiliary reports, special media or announcements that will be included on the coming Sunday, and who the point person will be. Remember that if Monday is tough for you, it is worse for the preaching pastor. (NOTE: never ask for a raise on Monday.)

Tuesday is a good day to debrief the prior Sunday. Ask your pastor questions like "were the services what you hoped or envisioned?" or "did the services accomplish what you had anticipated?" Take notes, and don't be defensive. Don't be too hard on yourselves regarding the technical issues; you are basically putting on a live production each week. These difficulties and unavoidable pitfalls are the very reasons that Television shows are now taped, rather than broadcast live. Next, ask your pastor to look forward to the coming Sunday. Do this humbly and gently, with nothing set in stone. Some good phrases include "how can I help enhance your message?" or "what tone would you like set before you speak?" What you're really saying is "how can I make you more successful?" Listen to the ideas and suggestions, and write them down. This is the submissive part of your role. Then, since you have spent the prior Thursday brainstorming the coming weekend, be prepared to show what you have "tentatively" planned, and the various elements that others have scheduled for that day. Give any input in the form of an additional idea, rather than a demand.

After this meeting of the minds, flesh-out the plan you began last Thursday: service theme, songs, keys and transitions. Arrange or modify any music that needs to be adjusted. Notify or confirm service participants and musicians regarding any special rehearsals or report times. This is also a good day to consider any aesthetic changes. See if there any simple changes in the appearance of the sanctuary or campus that will contribute to corporate worship.

Wednesday is a good target to finalize preparations for Sunday. Get the necessary information to the bulletin; make service cue sheets (discussed later); organize and arrange sheet music; plan and prepare for rehearsals; arrange for any projected lyrics, and try to anticipate all other details for the weekend. Please note that this weekly cycle is not intended to represent all that the Worship Leader does. It completely omits staff meetings and other pastoral care duties. It is merely designed to help deal with an otherwise relentless set of deadlines. Anticipating everything for Sunday is impossible, but if you have a plan, you will be less frustrated.

Planning—The Worship Service

Preparing the music, lyrics, media, aesthetics and participants must be a part of the Worship Leader's weekly routine, as was mentioned above. The Worship Leader must now coordinate the singers, instrumentalists, pastors, media and lay people to insure each knows their place and function in the flow of the service. Most churches have developed an organic cue sheet that has been developed for their particular needs.

A second option is to utilize one of the many online planning programs now available on the worldwide web. An online planning program is a centralized place to list and store public information including media, songs, schedules, rehearsal times, participants, stage layout, etc. both for services and for the entire church. Each church pays a fee to gain access to a variety of templates. One of the many advantages includes the ability of worship participants to access the service plan well in advance of the service. Additional advantages include the attachment of music, mp3 files, media notes and instant communication, to name a few.

There are some considerations when choosing an online planning program. The monthly price is often contingent on the size of the church, and on the services desired. Look into the availability of tutorials, and ask other users about the learning curve for both church staff and volunteers. If the program is not intuitive, it will not be utilized. Connectivity to email, mobile phone and networking sites is also important. Mp3, document storage, and expandability are additional considerations. A partial list of available websites and comparisons can be found in Appendix 4.

Planning—The Rehearsal

People participate in performing ensembles for a variety of reasons. Some want to offer their art as their sacrifice to God, while others are simply lonely and need to belong to something. Still others may need to escape their home-life for a bit. Life is difficult for many people, and a rehearsal should be a joy, not a burden. This may be the only opportunity some have to laugh, so be sure to laugh—a lot. Pastor your group by setting aside time for Scripture, prayer and some body life. A ten-minute time of Scripture and prayer is sufficient. What you lose in rehearsal time will be more than compensated for in the resulting unity. For a DVD of 4-minute video devotionals with accompanying questions, see the *Exploring Worship* DVD in Appendix 19.

Plan your rehearsal to the minute. Thoroughly planning your rehearsals will increase your productivity, and will let people know that you value both them and their time. Plan and post your rehearsal order. Have all the music ready, and build the expectation that your people will put their music in order before rehearsal begins. Plan the pace of the rehearsal to alternate between intense work and lighter moments. Start and end on time, no matter what. If your group performs a featured special song each week, the following guidelines will help prepare them. Have at least six features in the queue, representing a variety of styles and difficulties. A good rehearsal order and guideline is the following (song 1 = this week's special; song 6 is the newest):

Rehearsal Order	Notes & Actions
Warm-Ups	Keep it short. Focus minds & ears.
Welcome & Prayer	Focus hearts on the task. Take note of who is missing.
Song 2	Work nuance: phrasing and dynamics.
Song 1	Perfect, and work memorization if necessary.
Break	Choir leadership gives announcements & upcoming dates.
Song 3	Run-through, spot-rehearsing difficult or sloppy passages.
Song 4	Review past work, and then drop into context of the whole piece.
Song 6	Sight-read, point out difficulties, read again and put away.
Break	Devotions, care and prayer.
Song 5	Pick 2 to 3 difficult sections and break them down for success.
Song 1	Final run-through of the upcoming weekend's song.
Benediction	Send your people out with a blessing.

Planning—The Year

As inconvenient as it is to stop and plan, it is more painful not to plan, because it leaves a Worship Leader scrambling. If a leader will pay the price of planning twice per year, they can spend the other fifty weeks executing their plan, and ministering to the Church. Set aside one week in June, and one week in October. As dreams, music and ideas come across your desk during the year, place them into a file for consideration during your planning sessions. Also, stewardship of the church's musical instruments and technical equipment is often assigned to the Worship Leader, and it is essential to protect this investment. Schedule instrument maintenance and technological updates and checks during these weeks. Also, be sure to budget for repair, maintenance and replacement. See Appendix 13 for more help in this area.

In June, peruse and purchase music for September through January, remembering to consider special holidays, Missions emphasis weeks, additional events and extra services. These might include Thanksgiving Eve and Sunday, Christmas Eve and Advent. Include the choosing and planning of musical presentations, if this is part of your church's holiday expectation. Also consider planning something special for the first Sunday of the year. In the wake of the holiday season this Sunday can be an emotional letdown, and something special will give people a bit of a lift.

In October, take a week to again examine any new songs and ideas that you have filed for this purpose. Plan for February through June, remembering to include planning for Lent and Easter. Some churches also acknowledge special days like Mother's Day, Independence Day, and Veteran's Day. Again, include the choosing and planning of any musical presentations expected or desired. Attempt to give your large groups four to six weeks off during the summer.

For a vocal ensemble that sings each week, plan to purchase thirty pieces, and reuse twenty pieces (after building your music library for a few years). It is important to write down the date when a piece is performed. If a seasonal musical/cantata is to be performed, try to use at least four pieces from the concert as a lead up to the performance. This will save money, and help prepare your group to perform well. See Appendix 13 for more help in this area.

Planning—The Big Event

Administrative skills are never tested more than when putting on a large event. The most important point of an event is to know how it fits into the church's mission statement. "If you know the why, you can always figure out the how."[4] Most event organizers use what is called a "pert" chart (see Appendix 5), which will help the coordinator to accomplish a multitude of tasks in an organized and orderly fashion. Essentially, the planning starts with the end product, and works backward. Decide on the date(s), and room(s), and secure these on the church calendar, as well as with other ministries and committees. Give the participants plenty of advance notice, including extra rehearsals and performances. Be sure to include any sound and technical personnel requirements. When these major details have been addressed, progress to the event peripherals such as parking, printing, promotion, etc. A promotional plan is included in Appendix 6, and a sample Press Release is included in Appendix 7.

---

1 Hugh Ballou, *Moving Spirits, Building Lives* (Morris Publishing: Kearney, NE, 2005), 47.
2 Ballou, *Moving Spirits, Building Lives*, 52.
3 Ballou, *Moving Spirits, Building Lives*, 52.
4 Unknown

Chapter Eighteen

Leadership Skills

God works through leaders (e.g. Abraham; Moses; the Prophets; Jesus; Peter; Paul; etc). One can discern whether a person is a leader simply by observing whether they are being followed. Having followers does not make a person a *good* leader; merely a leader. A leader without a destination, for example, is simply taking a walk. In contrast, an effective leader is discerned by whether their followers get to the correct destination with the dignity with which God has imbued them.[1] This type of leadership demands selflessness and a genuine love for those who follow. Biblical leadership is best described as servanthood. With this concept as our guiding and restraining principle, we will examine the applicable wisdom of the corporate world. The following is a brief review of a few business leadership books that contain pertinent principles to the Worship Leader.

Principles of Leadership

Our first leadership book, *StrengthsQuest*, states that top achievers build on their talents.[2] Several definitions and principles carry over to our interest in worship leading. A *talent* was defined as "a naturally recurring pattern of thought, feeling, or behavior that can be productively applied."[3] A *theme* was, essentially a "group of similar talents."[4] This is relevant because of the multifaceted combination of musicianship, pastoral activities and public speaking skills that are employed in becoming a Worship Leader. A student with one skill group who is completely void of the accompanying skill group will not be successful in leading the Body of Christ in corporate worship, and will either have to utilize others, or serve in another position.

I substituted "effective leaders" for the book's "effective achievers" and gleaned these summary statements:

> Effective leaders *recognize* their talents and *develop* them into strengths.
> Effective leaders *apply* their strengths in roles that best suit them.
> Effective leaders *invent* ways to apply their strengths to their tasks.

In other words, Worship Leaders should find ways to develop and minister through their strengths and gifts. Conversely, they should discern their natural weaknesses and attempt to neutralize them. Weaknesses may never become strengths, but should at least be improved to the point that they will not undermine a person's ministry. This can be done through self-discipline, training, and by surrounding oneself with people whose gifts compliment your own.

A second leadership resource is Max DePree's book *Leadership is an Art*. DePree was the CEO of Herman Miller, a Fortune 500 company. This book has some excellent exhortations regarding a leader's need to work through others (an important concept when addressing the topic of worship teams or staff relations). While acknowledging the obligation to provide the services for which their organization has employed them, Mr. DePree also believes that *why* and *how* leaders get results are equally important. He defines the art of leadership as "liberating people to do what is required of them in the most effective and humane way possible."[5] His comments are constantly sprinkled with respect for, and inclusion of, the individual.

DePree takes great care to define the responsibilities of a leader, but his best contribution to the topic of worship leading is that a leader must be "abandoned to the strengths of others, admitting that we cannot know or do everything."[6] This bears a marked similarity to the biblical mandate given to pastors and teachers. Church leaders are not to *do* the work of the ministry, but rather to *equip* or prepare God's people to do it, so that the Body of Christ will be built up (Eph. 4:11–13). This concept must be especially underscored to people who may be seeking a Worship Leadership position in order to satisfy their own desire to perform.

Many Churches are experiencing change in the area of worship, and so-called "Worship Wars" are a reality in many congregations. A book called *Leading Change* addresses the causes of resistance to change, and how leaders can effectively overcome that resistance.[7] *Leading Change* notes that true change in societies and organizations is rare, and never comes readily. It suggests that change is usually a response to outside pressures, and is sometimes caused by social learning (or simple timing), but is rarely the result of leadership (that's the bad news). It asserts that all organizations have "a predisposition to tradition and conservatism"[8] or they would lapse into chaos and collapse. The author's formula for leading change begins with the leader convincing "the people with power of the rectitude of the proposed change."[9] (Note that the "people with power" may not hold a formal position in your Church. They may merely exert influence over the leadership, or perhaps are influential in their peer group. Whatever the case, you must know who has power in your particular congregation.) Next, says the author, the leader must demonstrate how the proposed change is a "necessary step toward progress"[10] as defined by those people with power. The author refers to this type of leadership as values-based leadership.[11]

Values-based leadership has particular relevance to Worship Leaders. The basis on which Worship Leaders institute change must be for the good and growth of the Body of Christ, rather than simply trying to keep pace with a constantly moving "cutting edge." Regarding "change," it should be stated that it is both impractical and an unworthy goal to change things merely for the sake of being different. Occasional change, however, provides the opportunity to educate worshippers, and to infuse their actions with significance. Upon returning to the familiar, it, too, will have taken on new meaning.

A maturing Church must be our core value and motivation, rather than change for personal taste or change for the sake of change. Leadership is a calling from God, and carries with it both a personal and a public obligation.

The Privilege of Leadership

In light of the privilege of Christ's invitation to lead, a few words of warning are timely. First is the reminder that an employee of the local church is feeding him/herself, and his/her family, from the very altar of God. The People of God have given tithes and offerings (their coined sweat; negotiable time and talent) to show their love for, and dependence on, God. These sacrifices are something holy (set apart) and must be received not only with deep gratitude, but also with reverence and a bit of holy fear. It was written about the sons of Eli: "... *the* sin of the young men was very great in the LORD'S sight, for they were treating the LORD'S offering with contempt."[12] Additionally, the person who uses these offerings in the execution of their job must be a careful and responsible steward.

Secondly, with a pastoral position often comes an undue amount of honor, and worse, power. The saying "power corrupts, and absolute power corrupts absolutely" is a fair warning to stay accountable and vulnerable. A second saying is like it: "those who seek power are unworthy to have it." Contrary to former pastoral models taught in seminaries, a pastor should not keep a safe distance from the congregation. Author and Priest Henri Nouwen notes that there is no "safe distance" from those we lead . . . That becomes a subtle way of exercising power over others.[13] He says that relevance and ability should take a back seat to vulnerability,[14] and that the future Church Leader must show that God "loves us not because of what we do or accomplish, but because God has created and redeemed us in love, and has chosen us to proclaim that love as the true source of all human life."[15]

The writer to the Hebrews states that pastors can deal gently with "the ignorant and misguided, since he himself also is beset with weakness."[16] Pastors should live, walk, pray, confess, and work in the midst his/her people. They do not deserve special privilege, and are not exempt from any regular responsibilities (King David stayed home from war, and look where it got him—2 Samuel 11). When your people tell you how wonderful you are, do not believe it. Do not read or believe your own press! People often idealize the pastoral position, and forget that you are made of the same fouled DNA as they. Err on the side of humility, and draw joy from pleasing God only (the Church does not need another money or sex scandal). Be reminded that God can speak through a jackass if he so chooses (Num. 22:28). He does not need you; he has merely extended to you the privilege of building His Kingdom. Christ chose you; you did not choose Christ (Jn. 15:16).

---

1 DePree, Max *Leadership is an Art* (New York, New York: Bantam Doubleday Dell Publishing Group, Inc.: 1989), 1.
2 Donald O. Clifton and Edward "Chip" Anderson, *StrengthsQuest* (Washington, D.C.: The Gallup Organization, 2003), 11.
3 Ibid., 6.
4 Ibid., 7.
5 DePree, Max *Leadership is an Art* (New York, New York: Bantam Doubleday Dell Publishing Group, Inc.: 1989), 1.
6 Ibid., 9.
7 O'Toole, James *Leading Change* (New York, New York, Ballantine Books; 1996), 153–254.
8 Ibid., 254.
9 Ibid.
10 Ibid.
11 Ibid., 8.
12 1 Sam. 2:17
13 Nouwen, 61–62.
14 Ibid., 30.
15 Ibid., 30.
16 Heb. 5:2

Chapter Nineteen

A Theology Of Technology

This chapter was distilled and adapted from a thesis presented by Mr. Drew Walsh in partial completion of the Master of Arts in Pastoral Studies, Worship Leadership degree, Azusa Pacific University. The experiences, research and observations are Drew's. I accept responsibility for its presentation herein.

Introduction

About 4 months ago I (Drew Walsh) attended a large, well-known megachurch in the Southern California area. Walking into the worship center, I knew this was going to be a unique experience. Volunteers handing out earplugs greeted me. Indeed, the music flowing from the double doors was already incredibly loud, and the service had not even begun! I proceeded to good seat, front and center, sure to catch all the action. As the service began, action was certainly what I saw.

My brain, desperately trying to multitask all the elements around me, switched back and forth so quickly I could barely keep up. The fifteen minutes of chaotic exchange that this church dubbed "worship" was interpreted by my brain to resemble something like this:

- *Engage in musical worship. SWITCH.*
- *Quickly shove in earplugs. SWITCH.*
- *Return to engage in musical worship. SWITCH.*
- *Notice a cool looking moving background. SWITCH.*
- *Return to engage in musical worship. SWITCH.*
- *Notice the lighting becoming more pronounced by the fog machine. SWITCH.*
- *Drawn back to the music by a guitar solo. SWITCH.*
- *Notice that the tech volunteer is a bit behind switching the lyric slides. SWITCH.*
- *Return to engage in musical worship. SWITCH.*
- *Attempt to concentrate despite the background music as you try to thank God for His work on the cross and the significance of each element. SWITCH.*

- *Invited to eat the bread and drink the juice of communion. SWITCH.*
- *Return to engage in musical worship. SWITCH.*
- *Notice the visual art going on to the side of the stage. SWITCH.*
- *Return to engage in musical worship. SWITCH.*
- *Notice the worship Twitter feed at the top of the projection screen. SWITCH.*
- *Get out cell phone to tweet a praise. SWITCH.*
- *Notice a new text message. SWITCH.*
- *Refocus to tweet a praise. SWITCH.*
- *Return to engage in musical worship. SWITCH.*

Multitasking

Sound a bit overwhelming and busy? This church did not think so. It seems that the ability to multitask was an expected and required skill for attendees. In truth, the term "multitasking" is a misnomer. It was originally a computing term, never intended to describe the way humans operate. The original definition referred to the "apparent simultaneous performance of two or more tasks by a computer's central processing unit. The word 'apparent' in the definition is very important. Just like your brain, the computer can't really focus on two or more things at the same time. In reality, the processor is switching rapidly between one program and the other, giving the illusion that it's doing it all at the same time."[1] When people refer to the act of multitasking they are actually speaking of *switchtasking*—the attempt to toggle between two or more undertakings.

According to David Crenshaw, the problem with multitasking—or should I say switchtasking—is that "anytime you switch from one activity or thought process to another, there is a cost."[2] This creates quite a challenge for the Church, which hopes to engage as many people as possible for as long as possible, while at the same time attempting to be relevant to the society in which it exists. While the motivation to engage worshipers is worthy, the Church must discern the potential side effects, both positive and negative, on those gathered.

Observations on Technology

Technology is a great thing, and can contribute much to the teaching and facilitating of worship in the corporate setting. Some of the many uses include:

- Projecting Scripture on which to meditate
- Projecting requests or various topics for which to pray
- Playing videos of confession and calls to worship
- Project readings, lyrics and corporate responses
- Immediate feedback and response from PDA's
- Exposure to Missionaries in the field
- Texting prayer-requests to those whose job it is to pray for worshipers

Beyond Sunday, technology can be used to equip, train, and facilitate. Some practical examples are to:

- Use social networking to facilitate prayer amongst church members
- Announce opportunities for service in the community and/or abroad
- Send weekly church-wide emails containing Scripture to memorize
- Direct church members to a blog that provides a Bible reading schedule and daily or weekly Scriptures on which to meditate

These are just a few of the many current uses, but as technologies increase, the opportunities for equipping church members will grow exponentially. Regardless of the methods, technology should contribute to the Church's calling to make and grow disciples, rather than becoming an end in itself.

As with any developing discipline, there are potential obstacles to the goals of worship and discipleship. One possible impediment is that the use of simultaneous media can be distracting which, in turn, can cause a congregation's depth of involvement and connection to suffer. Humans simply cannot tweet, sing, and participate in the Eucharist at the same time. One or more of these worshipful elements will suffer. Clergy may think otherwise, but multitasking during worship is a myth, nothing more. Worshipers will never be able to overcome the inherent constraints brought upon the switchtasking brain.

A second technological caution for a Church is that technology is highly formative in that it can either inspire praise, or create spectators. Without wisdom and theological guidance, it can distract rather than engage worshipers. For example, when an individual employs personal technology (tweeting, etc.), the result can be a fragmented, piecemeal offering to God. Finally, excessive amounts of technology can feed the rampant consumerist nature of our culture, producing "me-focused" worshippers. Technology should and must facilitate the actions and sacrifices of a congregation, or it will result in the individualization and depersonalization of a very corporate activity.

A Theology of Technology

Technology should be employed with purpose and direction, and should reflect the mission and values of the particular church and worship ministry. If your church strives to be missional in its gatherings, then technology should support that goal. If your worship ministry strives to create interactive communal experiences, then that objective should be accurately represented in the technologies employed. One path to purposeful technology is to assemble an organized set of goals for your Church's use of technology. Specific goals will help leadership better discern the appropriateness of certain medias, and will enable a fair and appropriate evaluation. Additionally, it will create a more stable, focused, and unified technology ministry.

Corporate Worship—Corporate Purpose

Technology should encourage and enhance the corporate expressions of the People. It should facilitate corporate response by creating opportunities for *communal* action, as opposed to *individual* action. Further, technology must focus and direct hearts toward God, rather than distract them; its contributions to worship must heavily outweigh its potential distractions. Technology, if used correctly, should allow for the still, small voice of God to be heard, facilitating times for hearts and minds to be quieted—a discipline so foreign to this culture.

Guidelines

First, try to keep worship multitasking to a minimum. This may mean employing fewer simultaneous media, in order to be more intentional about your use of technology. Remember that multitasking (switchtasking) is a myth! God doesn't deserve our piecemeal time; He deserves focused, first-fruit offerings. Second, technologies should only be employed if there are well-trained volunteers or staff who use them well. Poorly operated technology (i.e. lighting employed with poor taste; ill-timed slide transitions; poor choice of visual backgrounds; bad front-of-house mix; etc.) distracts worshippers. Thirdly, just because you have the technology does not mean it should be used, especially if it cannot be used well. Value purpose above "relevancy."

Evaluation

Technology is best evaluated through a retrospective lens. Because of the speed with which technology changes, periodic evaluations are necessary. Here is a partial list of questions for evaluation:

>Has this technology facilitated peoples movement through the service?
>How have people responded to this particular technology's use?
>Is this technology proving to be worth our time, money and personnel?
>Are these technologies being operated in an accurate and non-distracting manner or do the volunteers require more training?[3]

For more discussion, information and resources, visit Drew's blog and site at http://unceasingworship.wordpress.com/

---

1 David Crenshaw, *The Myth of Multitasking: How "Doing It All" Gets Nothing Done* (San Francisco Jossey-Bass, 2008), 30–31.
2 Ibid., 20.
3 Table 4: "Qualities of a Tech Steward" as found on website; http://unceasingworship.com

Chapter Twenty

Getting The Job

Many books have been written on how to interview for a job, yet none will fully prepare a person for the task. The all-important combination of calling, cultural fit, and chemistry with the Sr. Pastor are neither easily discerned nor casually found. The interview process differs from church to church, and your initial interview may be with a committee, rather than the Sr. Pastor. Do your best not to be desperate for work when interviewing with a Church. Likewise, try not to interview with a Church that is desperate; there may be a reason. Even if everything seems to point towards a successful conclusion, the best scenario for long-term success may be a three-month trial period.

Before the Interview

Do your research on the church, the pastor, the culture of the area, and on the church's reputation. A good starting place is the church's website, but remember that this is only one piece of the puzzle. Remember also that there are no perfect churches! You are simply gathering facts as you discern whether God is calling you to work in this particular "garden." Seek to have the character to refuse a job that pays too much for one's own good, or one where the work is too easy, or too prominent. Settle for nothing less than the call of God. A beautiful location and a good salary will feel ugly and impoverished if you are not where you belong.

    Anticipate the questions that are likely to be asked in the interview, and write down your answers to those questions. Know the musical style of the church, and be able to discuss your own style. Pastors do not generally know how to talk to a Musician so don't use a lot of musical terminology. Just a hint; if the Sr. Pastor is an ex-Worship Leader, think twice about the job, as they rarely let go of their past. Have a list of questions you want to ask sometime during the process. Remember that you are also interviewing them, but be respectful. Try to formulate a question that the pastor or committee is not expecting. This is where you will hear the unadulterated story. For a list of common interview questions, and job opening websites, see Appendix 8.

The Interview

Dress one level better than the interviewers. Observe everything when you enter the interview; how the are people dressed, their ages and gender, etc. If the interview is held in the Sr. Pastor's office, look at the pictures, books, trophies, diplomas, size and style of desk, type of computer. Listen carefully to the questions, and look people in the eye when listening or answering. Ask permission to ask some questions of your own. Take notes, tell the truth, and trust the Holy Spirit.

A Short Anecdote

Years ago, this author sensed the call of God to lead music and worship at a particular church. I went to the church service that Sunday, and as I was leaving, the associate pastor singled me out and introduced himself. I blurted out that I felt I was supposed to be the next music person at the church, and his response was "that's funny; our former person just resigned last week." The interview was arranged. Although I was a devoted Christian and an accomplished instrumentalist, I had little experience with churches or vocal music. After asking about my testimony and education, the interview went something like this:

> Do you sing?
>   No.
> Have you directed a choir before?
>   No.
> Have you sung in choirs?
>   Only as a kid; I hated it.
> Have you ever led singing?
>   No.
> Do you play the piano?
>   No.
> You've got the job!
>   I know. Thank you.

The power of the Holy Spirit cannot be overstated! I spent 15 happy and productive years there. The ministry grew to utilize a 100-voice choir and 25-piece volunteer orchestra every Sunday. We all learned together, and our love for and trust in each other was wonderfully contagious.

Conclusion

Churches are living, breathing organisms, and experience a variety of life cycles. The pastoral musician should not use the local church as a stepping-stone to bigger and better things. He or she must live and serve as though they will spend the rest of their days at that particular church. This attitude will keep a person from burning bridges or staying aloof from their people. Taking the long view is the best way to grow a people, and getting to see a generation of people grow to take their place in the Kingdom of God is completely fulfilling.

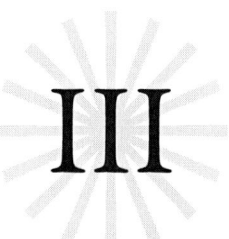

III

Towards An Understanding Of Symbolic Action

A person must learn to rest well with paradox to study the sacred actions of the Church, because Christianity is full of paradox. For example, Christ is 100% Man and 100% God. Whenever one is emphasized over the other, we depart from orthodoxy and distort His person. Mystery also applies to the Godhead, Who is both transcendent and immanent; above all, yet not removed; next to, yet not common; beneath all, yet not suppressed; within all, yet not contained.

James White defines the principle of sacred action (sacraments) as tangible things that are used to make spiritual things present.* Sacred actions, then, are a way for humans to commune with an invisible God, enabling the finite to live in relationship with the Infinite.

An Introduction to Sacramental Theology

✥✥✥

Baptism

✥✥✥

Communion

An Introduction to Sacramental Theology

Why should a Worship Leader care to learn about the Sacraments? The answer is that whether or not one believes Baptism and Communion impart grace, or merely symbolize what God has already done, a Worship Leader should be comfortable in speaking of intangible things. Baptism and Communion have always been an indispensable part of Christian piety and worship. However you think about and utilize these sacred actions, you should know and understand the ramifications of each point of view. Besides, you'll learn a lot about worship and people along the way.

Stop for a moment
and wrestle with the following questions:

What souvenirs do you find meaningful?

A picture? A trophy? A ring? A flag?
Are there any Christian symbols that are meaningful to you?
Does God do anything special during baptism and communion?
Must He?

✣ ✣ ✣

Does your church or fellowship have any symbols?

When does the use of a symbol become idolatry?

✣ ✣ ✣

Is there a meaningful place or action that makes you particularly aware of God's presence?

Do you feel you are acting most reverent when standing?
Bowing? Kneeling?
Does candlelight feel more mysterious than electric lights?
If so, why?

Chapter Twenty-One

An Introduction To Sacramental Theology

The incarnation of Jesus Christ is the event that will necessarily guide much of the consideration given to the topic of sacramental theology. The fact that God has enfleshed Himself in order to connect to His creatures gives permission, and perhaps precedent, for humans to respond in a similar way. The dangers of Sacred Actions and Symbols are well known: idolatry, form over spirit, repetition over response, and perhaps worst of all, apathy. Yet, Hebrews 1:3 states, "And He [Jesus] is the radiance of His glory and the exact representation of His nature."[1] In other words, as Andrew Hill stated, "Christ is the icon of God."[2]

As Christians attempt to worship in both Spirit and Truth (Jn. 4:24), they realize that "there is a physical side of being spiritual."[3] Robert Webber states, "The nature of faith demands the transformation of supernatural concepts into visible images and symbols."[4] Symbolism must be appropriated to communicate, because finite language cannot express supernatural truth. Evelyn Underhill notes that "In every human society which has reached even a rudimentary religious consciousness, worship is given its concrete expression in institutions and in ritual acts: and these institutions and acts become in their turn powerful instruments, whereby the worshipping disposition is taught, stimulated, and maintained."[5] She further explains that these 'concrete expressions' have a social quality, a two-fold quality (visible and invisible) and belong to two worlds (sense and spirit).[6] Human Beings employ rituals, signs and symbols in order to incarnate their response to God. Historically, many Christians have also believed that God participates in this communication in a special way through the performance of what are called "sacraments."

A problem inherent in expressing worship to a Being Who is wholly other-than is that Humans must use that-which-is-finite to express that-which-is-infinite. In his essay entitled "Transposition," C. S. Lewis describes the difference in these two realities as the difference between hearing an orchestral piece as it was intended, and then hearing it in its reduced state, played as a piano reduction. He observes "If the richer system is to be represented in the poorer at all, this can only be by giving each element in the poorer system more than one meaning."[7] Lewis' observations describe well the process of Sacred Action. In worship, Humans employ words, objects and elements that have an original intent or meaning, and then inject a fresh or representative significance into them. In this way, Humans are enabled to stand for a few moments at the intersection of time and eternity.

Ritual

Humans, however, do not want to stand at this intersection alone. Along with Underhill, Philip Pfatteicher notes, "Spirituality is usually marked by an awareness of other believers."[8] There appears to be a need or drive to experience this "otherness" with others of our own kind. This social aspect of worship reveals itself in the term "ritual," which the dictionary defines as "an established and prescribed pattern of observance, for example, in a religion."[9] Robert Webber offers a definition that is more on point: "a corporate symbolic activity in which people engage when they worship."[10] This corporate activity takes many forms. Liturgies are written, movement is prescribed, and sacred acts are performed.

"Liturgy" is a word with which the student of worship must become familiar. The Latin word *Leitourgia* roughly means "the work of the people." Orthodox theologian Alexander Schmemann defines it as "an action by which a group of people become something corporately which they had not been as a mere collection of individuals—a whole greater than the sum of its parts."[11] Liturgical activity is so central to a people's identity that one could not accurately study a culture without also examining its rituals.

Judaism, for example, is a religion that is rife with ritual. Its ancient tabernacle and temple rituals were detailed, and pregnant with meaning. Likewise, the calendar prescribed various sacrifices, festivals and remembrances that ordered Jewish life. Understanding these signs and symbols gives insight into the ancient practice of Judaism.

Sign and Symbol

Ritual almost always employs the use of signs and symbols. A 'sign' is "something that indicates or expresses the existence of something else not immediately apparent."[12] It does not usually look like what it represents; it points beyond itself. For example, when one sees the Nike logo, one is reminded of either the slogan ("just do it") or of the shoes themselves. Christian history has employed a variety of signs, and these signs were not always biblically based. Historic signs included marks of affiliation (the fish), prayer (hands), resurrection (the phoenix bird) and baptism (the scallop shell), among many others. These signs referred to or reminded people who "knew the code" of a certain piece of information.

A 'symbol' is different from a sign, and is defined as "something that stands for or represents something else, especially an object representing an abstraction."[13] The difference between a sign and a symbol is that a sign points to something, but does not resemble it. A symbol stands for, or represents, something. Leonard VanderZee states that "While the sign bears no necessary relation to that to which it points, the symbol participates in the reality of that for which it stands."[14] A symbol is like a stunt-double: it stands in for the real thing in order to represent the presence of that thing. Underhill notes, "A *symbol* is a significant image, which helps the worshipping soul to apprehend spiritual reality."[15] Orthodox theologian Alexander Schmemann portrays symbols as objects that manifest and communicate, rather than illustrate. He adds, "the symbol does not so much resemble the reality that it symbolizes as it participates in it, and therefore it is capable of communicating it in reality."[16]

It is at this point that the experience and knowledge of most students from the Free-Church tradition, including many Western Evangelicals, will begin to taper off. It is not the intention of this text to convince or transform a person's worship tradition, but rather, to inform people of an essential development in the history of worship and liturgy that has affected all Christian worship traditions in existence today. The study of Sacramental Theology is universally considered to be essential in the understanding of the development of historical Christian worship.

Sacrament

The necessity to employ the 'tangible to make the spiritual present' leads one naturally to the study and consideration of the concept of the sacrament. Though not in the Bible, this word has become essential to the understanding of historical worship and liturgy. The word originates from the Latin *Sacramentum*, and was originally a military term, referring to the oath of allegiance and obedience a soldier swore to his commanding officer. Author VanderZee notes, "Tertullian (b. about 160) first prominently used this term and applied it to the pledge of faith and allegiance made by candidates for baptism."[17] When the Bible was translated into Latin (the Vulgate) the word *Mysterion* was used to refer to the mystery of Christ's sacred actions. VanderZee mused as to whether the word was later applied to the sacraments because of a vague resemblance they have to some of the mysteries in the Greek religions.[18]

The concept of the sacrament adds an additional meaning to the use of sign and symbol: that of the dispensing of grace. Calvin stated, "A sacrament is a sign whereby God effects in us the promise that God signs and seals to us with that sign."[19] Augustine defined a sacrament as "a visible form of an invisible grace," but it was not all about the symbol for him. He believed, as did Calvin, that faith enabled people to receive grace through the sacraments, but that faith itself did not make the sacraments effective; only God did that. Augustine's famous dictum is "The word is added to the element and there results the sacrament."[20] Schmemann wrote, "A sacrament is both cosmic (embraces all of creation) and eschatological (oriented toward the kingdom which is to come)."[21] Donald Hustad states that a sacrament is "God's grace extended to human beings,"[22] while Underhill simply says "Symbols represent and suggest, whilst sacraments work."[23] In all definitions, God is the One who acts to give grace through the Sacraments. That, however, is where the similarities end. As we shall see upon examining both baptism and communion, each historical tradition has observed and interpreted the sacraments through a different lens.

A quick and simplified overview will initiate the student's thinking in these matters (giving just enough information to be dangerous), with more information to be added in the ensuing chapters. The Disciples of Jesus viewed the sacraments through the lens of being a participant in the Jewish new covenant (Jer. 31:31), while the Early Church looked through the lens of the Apostolic example. Later, the Orthodox tradition interpreted the Sacraments through the lens of the Divine Liturgy, while in the West, the lens was sacerdotal, meaning that the sacraments depended on the Priest (who exercises the power of the Church) to grant grace. In the Reformed tradition, the sacraments are viewed through the lens of prevenient grace, while the Anabaptist and Free-Church traditions view both baptism and communion as ordinances. Incidentally, there are a very few sects of Christianity (only Quakers and Salvationists), who do not observe the sacraments at all, as they believe these actions to be only and always spiritual, rather than tangible.

One important issue to be mentioned at the outset has to do with the term *Ex opere operato*, which means, "by the work being worked," or "done in the doing." As applied to Sacramental Theology, it means that the sacramental act produces the rendering of grace regardless of the faith of the recipient. This doctrine developed as an unfortunate side effect of Augustine's Doctrine of Original Sin during the 4th century, and led to the practice of grace being conferred upon any recipient, apart from conscious faith, thereby escorting the sacraments into both superstition and abuse.

One last differentiation must be made between the terms 'sacrament' and 'sacramental.' Schmemann notes that "a sacrament is primarily a revelation of the sacramentality of creation itself..."[24] Calvin suggests a good way to distinguish between what we will call the sacramental from a sacrament. "All created things are sacramental in the sense that as God's creation they point to, or signify, their Creator... A sacrament, however, is a particular created thing to which God attaches a word of promise."[25] By contrast, sacramental actions represent and suggest what is going on. In other words, sacraments do the work, while sacramental actions signify the work. Orthodox Christianity accepts both understandings.

---

*   James F. White, *Christian Worship in North American, A Retrospective: 1955–1995.* Collegeville, Minnesota: The Liturgical Press, 1997, 314.
1   *New American Standard Bible,* Update.(Copyright ©1960, 1962, 1963, 1968, 1971, 1972, 1973, 1975, 1977, 1995 by The Lockman Foundation; All rights reserved).
2   Taken from lecture notes on *Sign and Symbol* by Dr. Jack VanMarion, presented at the Institute of Worship Studies, January, 2005.
3   C.H. Pinnock, *Flame of Love: A Theology of the Holy Spirit* (Downers Grove, Ill: IV Press, 1996), 119, quoted in Anthony Cross and Philip Thompson, ed., *Baptist Sacramentalism* (Waynesboro, GA: Paternoster, 2003), 2.
4   Robert Webber (ed), *Twenty Centuries of Christian Worship: The Complete Library of Christian Worship,* Vol. 6 (Peabody Massachusetts: Hendrickson Publishers, Inc., 1994), 40.
5   Evelyn Underhill, *Worship* (Guildford, Surrey: Eagle, 1991 [orig. 1936]), 11.
6   Ibid., 16–19.
7   C. S. Lewis, *The Weight of Glory & Other Addresses* (San Francisco: Eerdmans, 1965 [orig., 1949]), 99.
8   Philip H. Pfatteicher, *Liturgical Spirituality* (Valley Forge, PA: Trinity Press, 1997), 5.
9   Encarta® World English Dictionary © 1999 Microsoft Corporation. All rights reserved. Developed for Microsoft by Bloomsbury Publishing Plc.
10 Webber, 139.
11 Alexander Schmemann, *For the Life of the World: Sacraments and Orthodoxy* (Crestwood, NY: St. Vladimir's Seminary Press, 1973), 25.
12 Encarta® World English Dictionary.
13 Encarta® World English Dictionary.
14 John E. Burkhart, "The Meaning and Mystery of the Sacraments," *Reformed Liturgy and Music* 29, no. 1 (1995): 7. Quoted in Leonard J VanderZee, *Christ, Baptism and the Lord's Supper* (Downers Grove, Illinois: IVP, 2004), 31.
15 Underhill, 33.
16 Alexander Schmemann, *The Eucharist: Sacrament of the Kingdom* (Crestwood, NY: St. Vladimir's Seminary Press, 1987), 38.
17 VanderZee, 28.
18 Ibid.
19 Ibid.
20 Augustine, *Tractates on the Gospel of John,* 80.3.4, 166.
21 Schmemann, *The Eucharist: Sacrament of the Kingdom,* 33.
22 Donald P. Hustad, *Jubilate II: Church Music in Worship and Renewal* (Carol Stream, IL: Hope Publishing Co., 1993), 186.
23 Underhill, 33.
24 Schmemann, *The Eucharist: Sacrament of the Kingdom,* 33.
25 VanderZee, 23.

Chapter Twenty-Two

Baptism In The Bible

A search for words related to baptism in the Bible will reveal no Old Testament references whatsoever. Still, it does appear that the Jews practiced baptism and ceremonial washing throughout the pre-Christian era. Ron Moseley, Ph.D. writes, "Dr. Merrill Tenney, the editor of the Zondervan Encyclopedia of the Bible, said, 'Baptism as a rite of immersion was not begun by Christians but was taken by them from Jewish and pagan forms. . . .'"[1] The pagan forms may have included baptismal practices from Zoroastrianism, a Persian religion to which the Jews were exposed during their exile in Babylon.

The Hebrews

Regarding Jewish forms of baptism, "Orthodox and Conservative Rabbis require both male and female conversion candidates to immerse themselves in a ritual bath called a mikveh. This ceremony is called tevillah."[2] Moseley notes, "Historically, we know that there were many ritual immersion baths (mikvaot) on the Temple Mount including one in the Chamber of Lepers situated in the northwest corner of the Court of Women (Mid. 2:5). Josephus, a Jewish historian, tells us that even during the years of war (66–73 A.D.) the laws of ritual immersion were strictly adhered to (Jos. Wars, 4:205). The Temple itself contained immersion baths in various places for the priests to use, even in the vaults beneath the court (Commentary to Tam. 26b; Tam. 1:1)."[3]

The Gospel Accounts

John the Baptizer appears in the opening account of each of the four Gospels. We can assemble a profile of the baptism of John by a quick survey of the various accounts. Matthew states, "Now in those days John the Baptist came, preaching in the wilderness of Judea" (3:1). Luke divulges the content of the Baptizer's preaching: "And he came into all the district around the Jordan, preaching a baptism of repentance for the forgiveness of sins" (3:3). Mark reveals the overwhelming public response, saying

"And all the country of Judea was going out to him, and all the people of Jerusalem; and they were being baptized by him in the Jordan River, confessing their sins" (1:5).

Though the act of baptism was not itself thought of as strange, John (the Gospel writer) does note that it aroused certain questions from the religious authorities. He writes, "They asked him, and said to him, 'Why then are you baptizing, if you are not the Christ, nor Elijah, nor the Prophet?'" (1:21), revealing that the Jews expected a variety of appearances to be associated with the coming of the Messiah. Though he did not fit neatly into their expectations, we learn that the Baptizer had been supernaturally appointed to baptize (1:33), and had been given a sign so that he would recognize the Christ. This reveals that, even though John and Jesus were half cousins, they must not have spent much post-womb time together (see Luke 1:36–44).

Besides calling for confession and repentance, we learn that John's baptism was an incomplete baptism. The Gospel writers all include statements of another baptism that was to follow John's: a baptism of "the Holy Spirit and of fire" (Matt. 3:11). Finally, we discern the purpose for which John had been sent to baptize. All four Gospel writers invoke the words of Isaiah the prophet regarding the Baptizer: "I am A VOICE OF ONE CRYING IN THE WILDERNESS, 'MAKE STRAIGHT THE WAY OF THE LORD,' as Isaiah the prophet said" (Jn. 1:23). John's role, then, was to help usher in the new and coming Kingdom of Heaven.

As the Gospels unfold, baptism continues to be a focal point. It is notable that after Jesus' baptism, John continued to baptize even though Jesus' disciples were also baptizing in the same general area (John 3). In this same chapter, Jesus makes an allusion to being born of "water and the spirit" (John 3:5) when explaining the new birth to Nicodemus. At the end of His earthly ministry, we hear Jesus' command that baptism was to be administered in the name of the Triune God (Matthew 28:19). In his account, Mark connects belief and baptism to salvation (Mark 16:16). Finally, Jesus appropriates the term "baptism" when referring to the process of his coming passion (Mark 10:39; Luke 12:50).

One question plagues all who consider baptism: "Why was Jesus baptized?" The Baptizer, himself, protests at the thought of baptizing the Christ (Matt. 3:14), and Jesus' rationale leaves much to speculation. He simply replies, "Let it be so for now; for thus it is fitting for us to fulfill all righteousness" (Matt. 3:15). VanderZee speculates that Christ's purpose in being baptized was to identify with sinners.[4] Others have wondered if Christ was exemplifying submission, humiliation or obedience. I tend to agree with Bridge and Phypers' perspective that Jesus was not a sinner, but in order to save sinners according to the purpose of God, He had to take his place alongside sinners. To the causal observer at least, Christ would have been completely indistinguishable from them.[5]

Apostolic Baptism

In the book of Acts the Gospel writer Luke strongly connects baptism to repentance. He documents that Peter first administered Christian baptism during the Jewish Pentecost celebration. Peter had preached publicly, employing John the Baptizer's words "repent and be baptized," connecting baptism to the washing away of sins (2:38; 22:16). A cursory reading of the book of Acts reveals that baptism seems to be the first and most natural step after receiving forgiveness. It was withheld from no one who repented, regardless of race, status or gender.

Both Peter and Paul used baptism to interpret and apply biblical history. Peter, in speaking of salvation, refers to the story of Noah, writing,

> . . . when the patience of God kept waiting in the days of Noah, during the construction of the ark, in which a few, that is, eight persons, were brought safely through *the* water. Corresponding to that, baptism now saves you—not the removal of dirt from the flesh, but an appeal to God for a good conscience—through the resurrection of Jesus Christ (1 Peter 3:20–21).

In like manner, Paul speaks of baptism as an escape, this time from bondage, when he refers to Moses and the Egyptians at the Red Sea, stating "For I do not want you to be unaware, brethren, that our fathers were all under the cloud and all passed through the sea; and all were baptized into Moses in the cloud and in the sea" (1 Corinthians 10:1–2). In referencing baptism, these two Apostles help to form the young Church's understanding and use of baptism.

Bath, Burial and Birth

The ritualistic use of water in the New Testament alternately refers to a **bath** (sanctifying), a **burial** (destroying/redemption) or a **birth** (salvation/life-giving). Biblical examples can be categorized as follows:

Bath (Sanctification)
  - A sign of repentance or ritual cleansing (Luke 3:3; 1 Corinthians 6:11)
  - Preparation for the Messiah (John 1:23)
  - A sign of belief (Colossians 2:12)

Burial (Redemption)
  - Death to self (Romans 6:3–4)
  - An escape from bondage (1 Corinthians 10:1–6)
  - Unites to the death of Christ (Romans 6:3–4)

Birth (Salvation)
 - New birth (John 3:5–7)
 - Entrance into the new covenant (Colossians 2:12)
 - Initiation into the Christian Community (1 Corinthians 12:13)

The way in which a particular Church body views baptism will both reflect and form their view of the Christian life. In our day, one could peruse each denomination's baptism practices and draw conclusions regarding that Church's outlook on both salvation and piety.

The Water-Spirit Connection

There are numerous references throughout the Epistles that may also refer to baptism. Words and phrases like "washing," "cleansing," "dying to self" etc. are often interpreted as having baptismal connotations. Since these references are a bit more open to interpretation, they have not been included in this general overview. The reader, however, will recall that John the Baptizer knew his baptism to be incomplete, stating that the Christ would "baptize with the Holy Spirit and with Fire" (Matt. 3:11). Examples of this connection between water baptism and Holy Spirit baptism are, therefore, too important to neglect herein.

In the story of his conversion experience, water and spirit are linked as Saul receives the Holy Spirit and is baptized (Acts 9:17–18). Again, at the house of Cornelius, the family receives the Holy Spirit and is baptized (Acts 10:44,47). At Corinth, Paul stumbles upon a group of heretofore unknown followers of Christ. They had repented and been baptized, but had not received the Holy Spirit. Paul then rebaptized them, and they immediately received the Holy Spirit (Acts 19:5–6). The connection of Spirit and water is also evident in 1 Corinthians 12:13, which says "For by one Spirit we were all baptized into one body, whether Jews or Greeks, whether slaves or free, and we were all made to drink of one Spirit." Finally, Titus 3:5 also makes this water-Spirit connection, stating, "He saved us, not on the basis of deeds which we have done in righteousness, but according to His mercy, by the washing of regeneration and renewing by the Holy Spirit." Whether the ritualistic use of water refers to sanctification, redemption or salvation, it always seems to be associated with work that only The Holy Spirit can do.

1 Ron Moseley, "The Jewish Background of Christian Baptism." Sherwood, Arkansas: Arkansas Institute of Holy Land Studies, 2002. Database online. Available from http://www.Haydid.org.html. Accessed 8 September 2006.
2 Advisory Board of the Conversion to Judaism Resource Center, Baptism—Jewish; Immersion Conversion to Judaism Resource Center. Database online. Available from http://www.convert.org/process.htm. Accessed 8 September 2006.
3 Ron Moseley, "The Jewish Background of Christian Baptism."
4 VanderZee, 80.
5 Donald Bridge & David Phypers. *The Water That Divides: A Survey of the Doctrine of Baptism* (Downers Grove, Illinois: Christian Focus Publications, 1998), 18.

Chapter Twenty-Three

Baptism Throughout History

Introduction

The word baptize (*baptizein* in Greek) means to submerge a cloth into dye in order to change its color. This connotation, in addition to the numerous references to baptism as burial, tells us that immersion is the logical mode of baptism. Still, this was probably not practical in all circumstances. For example, if people who lived during biblical times did not live near a river, immersion would have presented a great difficulty. Additionally, a situation such as the one recorded in Acts 2, where 3,000 people were converted and baptized, would not likely have been possible using the mode of immersion. Two other modes of baptism developed either during or directly following the Apostolic era. The second mode of baptism is called "affusion," and refers to the pouring of water over the head of the candidate, perhaps portraying the outpouring of the Holy Spirit that, as mentioned previously, was closely linked to water baptism. Affusion was usually performed with the candidate standing in water. The third baptismal mode is sprinkling, and is probably linked to the sprinkling of the blood of Christ (Hebrews 12:24 and 1 Peter 1:2).

It has been previously mentioned that the ritualistic use of water usually falls into the categories of "bath, burial or birth." An interesting way to discern how various Christians have understood the rite is to look at the design of their baptistry. Peoples who have understood baptism as a "bath" have generally constructed a rectangular baptistry, or have baptized in "living" i.e. running water. A "burial" interpretation of baptism often found expression in either a cruciform or hexagon-shaped baptistry. The six-sided baptistry correlated to the 6th day, the day on which Christ was crucified. The "birth" understanding of baptism produced either a round baptistry (probably representing the birth canal) or an octagonal design. The eight-sided baptistry drew a parallel to the 8th day, the day of resurrection, also known as the day of new creation.

Baptismal Practice in the Early Patristic Era

A brief review of early Church writings will provide a glimpse into the developing theology of baptism. The first and perhaps earliest document to be considered is the 1st century document *The Didache*, which purports to be "The Lord's Teaching Through the Twelve Apostles to the Nations." It states:

> And concerning baptism, baptize this way: Having first said all these things, baptize into the name of the Father, and of the Son, and of the Holy Spirit, in living water. But if you have no living water, baptize into other water; and if you cannot do so in cold water, do so in warm. But if you have neither, pour out water three times upon the head into the name of Father and Son and Holy Spirit. But before the baptism let the baptizer fast, and the baptized, and whoever else can; but you shall order the baptized to fast one or two days before. (Chapter 7)

> But let no one eat or drink of your Eucharist, unless they have been baptized into the name of the Lord; for concerning this also the Lord has said, "Give not that which is holy to the dogs." (Chapter 9)

Items of note include the invocation of the **Triune** God, the allowance of **affusion** and the **preparation** of the baptismal candidate (whereas no preparation was present in the New Testament). Of special interest is the fact that baptism **entitles** one to participate in the act of Communion.

The mid-2nd century document, *The First Apology* of Justin Martyr refers to baptism in chapters 61 and 65 as the means whereby men and women are dedicated to God and made new through Christ. It is given to as many as are persuaded and believe that the things are true which the Church teaches, and who undertake to live accordingly. It is preceded by prayer and fasting by both the candidates and the congregation. The candidates are then "brought where there is water and are born again, being washed in the Name of the Father, the Son and the Holy Spirit." Justin explains:

> But we, after we have thus washed him who has been convinced and has assented to our teaching, bring him to the place where those who are called brethren are assembled, in order that we may offer hearty prayers in common for ourselves and for the baptized [illuminated] person, and for all others in every place, that we may be counted worthy, now that we have learned the truth, by our works also to be found good citizens and keepers of the commandments, so that we may be saved with an everlasting salvation. Having ended the prayers, we salute one another with a kiss. (Chapter 65)

A significant development is the **process** in which a convert becomes a member of the Christian community. There were, in the mid-2nd century, four stages through which converts had to pass: 1) Seeker (energumens); 2) Hearer (illuminands); 3) Kneeler and Baptism; 4) Faithful (continuing). Only one half century after the last Apostle died, the Church had developed a required path toward initiation and piety. The reasons for this were probably a combination of Man's natural tendency to institutionalize and the intense persecution the Church was enduring at the time.

At the beginning of the 3rd century, the *Apostolic Tradition of Hippolytus* reveals the practice of the church in Rome, where baptism had evolved into a 3-year initiation process. Herein are the pertinent writings:

> On preparation for baptism: "Catechumens shall continue to hear the word for three years. But if a person is keen, and perseveres well in the matter, the time shall not be judged, but only his conduct. . . . When the teacher has finished giving instruction, let the catechumens pray by themselves, separated from the faithful . . . And when they have finished praying, they shall not give the Peace, for their kiss is not yet holy."

> And when those who are to receive baptism are chosen, let their life be examined: have they lived good lives when they were catechumens? Have they honored the widows? Have they visited the sick? Have they done every kind of good work? And when those who brought them bear witness to each: 'He has', let them hear the gospel.

> From the time that they were set apart, let hands be laid on them daily while they are exorcized. And when the day of their baptism approaches, the bishop shall exorcize each one of them, in order that he may know whether he is pure . . .

> Those who are to be baptized should be instructed to bathe and wash themselves on the Thursday . . . Those who are to receive baptism shall fast on the Friday. On the Saturday those who are to receive baptism shall be gathered in one place at the bishop's decision. They shall all be told to pray and kneel. And he shall lay his hand on them and exorcize all alien spirits . . .

> And they shall spend the whole night in vigil; they shall be read to and instructed. Those who are to be baptized shall not bring with them any other thing, except what each brings for the Eucharist. For it is suitable that he who has been made worthy should offer an offering then.

This baptism service was to eventually become the Easter Vigil, wherein candidates (catechumens) were baptized on Easter Sunday morning. The service began with prayer over the water at cockcrow. Candidates disrobed completely, including jewelry. Baptism was preceded by anointing with the oil of exorcism and prayer for the departure of spirits. A threefold baptism by immersion was then accompanied by interrogation and affirmation of belief in the clauses of the Apostles' Creed. The newly initiated Christian was then clothed, followed by a further anointing with the oil of thanksgiving, and the laying-on of hands by the bishop. They were then able to participate in the kiss of peace, and in a triple communion (bread with three cups). This lengthy initiation spotlights the significance of both the holy kiss and the Eucharist for the early Believers, and was probably motivated by the current persecutions by Rome.

Baptismal Understanding in the Late Patristic Era

Baptismal practices during the Early Patristic era evolved in both the **extent** of baptismal preparation and in the actual **administration** of the rite itself. During the Late Patristic era, a third development had to do with what the various Church Fathers **understood** to be happening during the rite. Though the formal schism would not take place for another 700 years, differences in understandings began to separate themselves into West (which would become Roman Catholic) and East (which would become the Orthodox church).

In the West, Ambrose of Milan (d. 397) described the process of baptism as a way for a living person to die and to rise again, stating, "the font is a kind of grave." He wrote:

> To break the hold of the devil in this world as well, a means was found for making a living man die and a living man rise again . . . [*in baptism*] the heavenly sentence is thus served, without the loss of consciousness involved in death. Because you are immersed, the sentence, 'You are dust and to dust you shall return', is served. With the sentence served there is room for the gift and the heavenly remedy . . . the conditions of life did not permit us to be covered by the earth and then rise again from it . . . so it is that *the font is a kind of grave.*

The Eastern understanding comes to us by way of Cyril, the 4th century Bishop of Jerusalem. He notes, "We are handing on to you a mystery, a hope of the Age to come. Guard the mystery from those who would waste this prize."[1] For Cyril and the East, baptism is not only a symbol of death and resurrection with Christ (taking place on Easter Sunday at a place believed to be the site of Christ's tomb), but also carried an eschatological meaning. He writes "Christ is here in your midst . . . He is ready, O you who want to be baptized, to bring you by the Holy Spirit into the presence of the Father."[2] A further development in the East was the importance of chrismation (anointing) and renunciation of the Devil. Cyril writes:

> That tyrant of old pursued the ancient Jewish people as far as the seas, and here and now the devil, bold and shameless, the source of all evil, followed you

up to the *waters of salvation*. Pharaoh was submerged in the sea, and the devil disappears in the *waters of salvation*.

Nonetheless, you are told to stretch out your hand, and to address the devil as if he were before you: I renounce you, Satan. I will tell you now, for you need to know, why you face westward. The west is the quarter from which darkness appears to us; now the devil is darkness, and wields his power in darkness. So we look to the west as a symbolic gesture, and renounce the leader of shadow and darkness.

An overview of baptism during the Late Patristic era would be neither possible nor complete without the contribution of the great Augustine of Hippo (354–430). His doctrine of Original Sin unwittingly birthed the sacramental principle of *ex opere operato* ("by the work being worked," or "done in the doing") and became the theological *modus operandi* throughout the entire Medieval period. The understanding that the outward action produces the fact of the inward change "developed quickly from about the time of Augustine, when the doctrine of original sin had become clearly formulated and widely accepted."[3] This continues to be the sacramental understanding of both Roman Catholicism and Eastern Orthodox.

Paedobaptism

Paedobaptism triggered the formulation of the doctrine of original sin. This term refers to the baptism of infants, and was an extant practice of the Patristic era. A short review is necessary in order to understand the circumstances of Augustine's arrival at this doctrine and its subsequent results. Origen (circa 185), commenting on Romans 6:5–7 (dealing with the likeness of Christ's death and resurrection) states, "For this reason the Church received from the Apostles the tradition of baptizing children too."[4] However, Tertullian (circa 205), while acknowledging the existence of the practice, expresses doubts about the wisdom of infant baptism. He writes, "It follows that deferment of baptism is more profitable, in accordance with each person's character and attitude, and even age: and especially so as regards children . . . All who understand what a burden baptism is will have more fear of obtaining it than of its postponement. Faith unimpaired has not doubt of its salvation."[5] Still, within 30 years of Tertullian's comments, infant baptism became the unquestioned rule for both the East and the West.

Augustine, then, inherited the custom of infant baptism as the standard practice, but wondered how it could be a baptism for repentance, since babies had not consciously sinned. His answer was to separate the conscious sin of adults from the inherited sin of Adam (see Romans 5:12–21 and 1 Corinthians 15:21–22), thus revealing two types of guilt; inherited sin and personal sin.

Thus, thought Augustine, the sacrament of baptism, when bestowed upon an infant, cleanses the infant of their inherited sin, clearing their way to heaven. In a time of high infant mortality, this must also have given great relief to grieving parents. Unwittingly, however, Baptismal Sanctification was born. Personal faith was taken out of the equation, leaving the ceremony itself to grant grace to the recipient. Infant baptism, then, found its rationalization in the doctrine of original sin after the fact. An unfortunate by-product of this doctrine was the concept of *ex opere operato*, where the sacraments could communicate grace apart from faith. Rather than starting with Scripture to form doctrine, Augustine, in this case, began with the accepted practice of infant baptism and then tried to proof text its existence. Though the Doctrine of Original Sin is widely accepted, *ex opere operato* is widely contested. This was not Augustine at his most Biblical.

Paedobaptism is still practiced for a variety of reasons. One perspective embraces the practice because it emphasizes the objective, preexisting fact of God's grace, rather than the subjective response of the baptized. "If Christ has redeemed Mankind," they say, "then the only requirement is membership in the sinful race of humanity, which infants also possess." A second explanation has to do with what is known as covenant theology. This interpretation does not separate the two testaments, but takes them as one continuous witness. Baptism, in this view, is a continuation of circumcision (Acts 2:39; Col. 2:11–12), where God included Hebrew infants in the blessings of His covenant. Baptism, then, is based on the child's birth into a covenant family; what one person described as a kind of "invisible tattoo that God puts on the infant."[6] Objections to this view include the fact that the candidate is missing both repentance and a profession of faith. VanderZee states "There are not two kinds of baptism, one for infants and one for adults, with different premises . . . if infant baptism cannot be supported on the same basis and with the same understanding as adult baptism, then it is unacceptable."[7] Paedobaptism continues to be an emotional issue even into the present day.

Baptismal Understanding in the Reformation

Martin Luther's understanding of the necessity of a personal faith led him to reject baptismal sanctification. Yet, he made allowance for infant baptism, because he believed it best expressed the true relationship of the sinner to God. He explains: "The sinner does not so much need to be washed as he needs to die, in order to be wholly renewed and made another creature, and to be conformed to the death and resurrection of Christ, with whom he dies and rises again through baptism."[8] He focused on the promise of God from Mark 16:16, which says "He who has believed and has been baptized shall be saved" which he took as a guarantee from God Himself. Pfatteicher notes, "Luther taught us not just to remember our baptism but to glory in it."[9]

Though Luther (1483–1546) was the main Protest-ant, many thought he did not take his protest far enough. The Anabaptists were one such group who felt the Reformation to be incomplete. They rejected paedobaptism, insisting instead upon a regenerated church membership. Zwingli (1484–1531), though not always associated with the Anabaptists, considered the acts of baptism and communion to be ordinances, rather than sacraments. "Ordinance is an alternate word used by many Protestants (especially Baptists) signifying baptism and communion to be acts which are ordained by Christ and are to be done within the community of the Church. Though Protestants, even today, use the word *sacrament* in the sense of a vow of loyalty, they don't mean that the acts convey grace apart from the faith of the individual. It is in this sense that R. S. Wallace defines a sacrament as a 'religious rite or ceremony instituted or recognized by Jesus Christ.'"[10] John Hammett defines the meaning of baptism as "representing or symbolizing the identification, purification and incorporation of the believer into the Body of Christ."[11] Objections to Ordinance Theology have generally centered on the fact that the sacred actions depend too much upon the work of Man rather than the work of God.

Calvin (1509–1564) was a second generation Protestant who attempted to take a mediating position between Luther and the Anabaptists. He built his Sacramental Theology upon the prevenient grace of God, contending that God's grace precedes both personal conversion and baptism. He states, "A sacrament is an external sign by which the Lord seals on our consciences His promises of goodwill toward us, in order to sustain the weakness of our faith, and we in turn testify our piety towards Him, both before Himself, and before angels as well as men."[12] Calvin accepted the practice of paedobaptism because it put God in the correct position as the grace-giver. He explains, "Infants of Christian parents are to be baptized for future repentance and faith, while unbaptized adults . . . are required to display signs of repentance and faith . . ."[13]

John Wesley (1703–1791) believed in a personal, subjective experience of conversion and pardon. He, as an unconverted Anglican priest, believed in baptismal regeneration (*ex opere operato*), but after his conversion, he arrived at a completely original understanding of baptism, which also allowed for his acceptance of paedobaptism. He suggested that in baptism "infants are born again of the Holy Spirit and cleansed from inherited sin. But as a matter of observed fact, each then grows into a life of personal sin, forfeiting their eternal life. Each then needs to be regenerated a second time by adult conversion."[14] Wesley accepted Augustine's doctrine of original sin, but with the caveat that one could lose their salvation, and must be regenerated once again through a subjective conversion experience.

Closing Thoughts

Each tradition brings a unique perspective to the act of baptism. Similarities are few, but there are some to considered. For example, baptism has always been considered the individual's initiation into the Body of Christ. It should therefore take place in the presence of the gathered believers, rather than in isolation. Additionally, in all times, baptism has represented either bath, burial or birth, with the design of the baptistry often revealing the People's beliefs concerning the rite.

---

1. *Catechetical lectures of Cyril of Jerusalem,* 9.79.
2. Bridge & Phypers, 14.
3. Ibid.
4. Jeremias, *Infant Baptism,* 65. Quoted in VanderZee, 127.
5. Tertullian, *De baptismo,* X III. 19–34. Quoted in VanderZee, 74.
6. In a lecture by Dr. Jack Van Marion during class 703 at the Institute of Worship Studies in Orange Park, Florida, 2004.
7. VanderZee, 121.
8. Martin Luther, *The Babylonian Captivity of the Church* (1520), Luther's Works 36.58, quoted in Pfatteicher, 234.
9. Pfatteicher, 235.
10. R. S. Wallace, "Sacrament," in Elwell, ed., *Evangelical Dictionary of Theology,* 1047. Quoted in John S. Hammett *Biblical Foundations for Baptist Churches* (Grand Rapids, MI: Kregal) 259.
11. Hammett, 264.
12. John Calvin, *Institutes,* IV. xvi, 21.
13. Bridge & Phypers, 123.
14. Bridge & Phypers, 140.

Chapter Twenty-Four

The Covenant Meal And Communion In The Bible

In the book of Leviticus, Moses received from the LORD (Lev 23) a mandate regarding what are called "holy convocations" (verse 4 ff). This list included Sabbath, the Passover, the Feast of Unleavened Bread, the Feast of First Fruits, Pentecost, the Feast of Trumpets (Rosh Hashanah, or the New Year), the Day of Atonement (Yom Kippur), the Feast of Huts, Sabbath Year, and the Year of Jubilee. These Feasts connected the worship of God with concrete historical events, provided annual opportunities for theological instruction, and often included a symbolic communal meal.

Three of the above-mentioned feasts were considered pilgrimage feasts because "every male Jew of twelve years and older was obliged each year to make the pilgrimage to Jerusalem for at least one of these feasts."[1] These particular festivals were connected to flocks or crops, and included Passover (which fused with the Feast of Unleavened Bread during the Exodus event), The Feast of Weeks (later called Pentecost) and the Feast of Huts. The additional feasts of Rosh Hashanah, Yom Kippur, Hanukkah and Purim were feasts that commemorated God's saving events.

The Covenantal Meal

The typical Jewish meal was far more than a mere nourishing necessity. It must be understood as an act of fellowship and acceptance; in its eating, a community was formed. The meal was also used as a covenant meal, and as such was integral in the sealing of a covenant. Psalm 23, for example, is exemplary in its covenantal language, listing the many benefits of making a covenant with the Shepherd-King, Jehovah-Raah (the LORD my Shepherd). Verse two of Psalm 23 speaks of being led to places of restful provision, while in verse three the subordinate is guided to successful living (leads in paths of righteousness). Verse five reinforces the Shepherd-King's presence and protection in dangerous places, and then describes a typical covenant meal between a vassal and his overlord (prepares a table in the presence of enemies).

The Gospel Accounts

Matthew, Mark and Luke all say that Jesus chose to institute his feast squarely on the first day of the Feast of the Passover, also known as the feast of Unleavened Bread (Matt. 26:17; Mark 14:12; Luke 22:7). The feast would no longer be simply a time to remember an event; it would now represent an entirely new covenant! The sacrificial undertones of this new feast are unmistakable, as this is also the day on which the Passover lamb was to be sacrificed. John's Gospel, however, is different from the synoptic Gospels (Matthew, Mark and Luke). In his account, John states that the supper happened "before the Feast of the Passover" (13:1). John focuses on the fact that, at this supper, Jesus washed his Disciple's feet. He does not even mention Christ's covenantal reinterpretation of bread and wine. This difference in timing is a small but curious inconsistency in the Gospel accounts. John, however, does mention with the others that Jesus exposes his betrayer at this supper. Also, the synoptic accounts of this covenant meal have an eschatological element, as each reports Jesus saying He will not drink wine again until He is rejoined with those present in his Father's kingdom.

During the supper, Jesus utilizes terms from the Jewish table blessing (*berakah*) as He distributes the elements of the covenant meal to the Disciples. The Synoptic accounts record Jesus' actions with the words "took; blessed; broke." Then He gave the bread to those at the table. Interestingly, John records the terms "took; blessed; gave" in his account of Jesus feeding the five thousand (6:11).

The institution of this new-covenant meal is best left to the words of Jesus himself.

> **Matthew 26:26** While they were eating, Jesus took *some* bread, and after a blessing, He broke *it* and gave *it* to the disciples, and said, "Take, eat; this is My body." 27 And when He had taken a cup and given thanks, He gave *it* to them, saying, "Drink from it, all of you; 28 for this is My blood of the covenant, which is poured out for many for forgiveness of sins."

> **Mark 14:22** While they were eating, He took *some* bread, and after a blessing He broke *it*, and gave *it* to them, and said, "Take *it*; this is My body." 23 And when He had taken a cup *and* given thanks, He gave *it* to them, and they all drank from it. 24 And He said to them, "This is My blood of the covenant, which is poured out for many."

Luke 22:19 And when He had taken *some* bread *and* given thanks, He broke it and gave it to them, saying, "This is My body which is given for you; do this in remembrance of Me." **20** And in the same way *He took* the cup after they had eaten, saying, "This cup which is poured out for you is the new covenant in My blood."

Interestingly, John also makes reference to the eating of the body of Jesus, and the drinking of His blood. In the previously mentioned account of the feeding of the five thousand (John 6), Jesus says "Truly, truly, I say to you, unless you eat the flesh of the Son of Man and drink His blood, you have no life in yourselves" (v. 53). Whether Jesus meant for the bread and wine to actually become his body, or merely to signify it, has led to much interpretation, division, superstition and abuse. It is the intention of this particular text to simply state what is, postponing the various interpretations until the final chapter in this section. Perhaps, however, the covenant that Moses ushered in will shed some understanding upon Jesus' reference to the blood of the covenant.

Exodus 24:5 He sent young men of the sons of Israel, and they offered burnt offerings and sacrificed young bulls as peace offerings to the LORD. 6 Moses took half of the blood and put *it* in basins, and the *other* half of the blood he sprinkled on the altar. 7 Then he took the book of the covenant and read *it* in the hearing of the people; and they said, "All that the LORD has spoken we will do, and we will be obedient!" 8 So Moses took the blood and sprinkled *it* on the people, and said, "Behold the **blood of the covenant,** which the LORD has made with you in accordance with all these words."

Jesus employs the words of Moses ("blood of the covenant") when instituting His new-covenant meal. Rather than a bull's blood, however, He would use his own blood, which would be represented in the new-covenant meal by wine. Whether this "last supper" was a Passover meal or simply a typical Jewish meal just before the Passover, there can be no misunderstanding that Jesus meant it to be a covenant meal, built on the foundation and imagery of the Passover Feast. Exodus 12 tells the story of the Israelites' deliverance and the utilization of both blood and bread. They are told in 12:14: "Now this day will be a memorial to you, and you shall celebrate it *as* a feast to the LORD; throughout your generations you are to celebrate it *as* a permanent ordinance."

This verse has two important words regarding the Feast. "Memorial" is from the Hebrew root word *zeker*, meaning "a memento; by implication, commemoration:—memorial, memory, remembrance, scent."[2] "Ordinance" is the second significant word for our purposes. It is from the Hebrew root *choq*, meaning "an enactment; hence, an appointment (of time, space, quantity, labor or usage):—appointed, bound, commandment, convenient, custom, decree(-d), due, law, measure, x necessary, ordinance(-nary), portion, set time, statute, task."[3] In this way, the Israelite was to use the Feast of Unleavened Bread to remember so as to reenact, as if they themselves had gone through the Red Sea. It is a remembering as though it were happening again.

Anamnesis is the Greek word for "remembrance" and means "recollection:—remembrance (again)."[4] When Jesus institutes His new-covenant meal based upon the Passover, He says, "do this in remembrance of Me" (Lk. 22:19), invoking the same kind of remembering which is applied to the Passover event. Regarding this remembrance and celebration of Passover, the Jewish Mishnah instructs, "in every generation a man must so regard himself as if he came forth himself out of Egypt . . . He brought us out from bondage to freedom." This new-covenant meal, then, is to be understood as an extension of the Feast of Unleavened Bread, where bread and wine are used as a way to personally participate in the event of deliverance through an active and reenacting type of remembrance.

Though John's Gospel does not include the actual words of institution, he clearly delineates both the **example** of the new covenant and the **stipulation** of this covenant. He records Jesus saying, "If I then, the Lord and the Teacher, washed your feet, you also ought to wash one another's feet. For I gave you an *example* that you also should do as I did to you" (13:14–15). At the supper, John witnesses the Initiator of the new covenant on his knees washing feet. The **stipulation** of this covenant is the command to love as He has loved, and is at the heart of this new-covenant meal. Jesus says, "A new commandment I give to you, that you love one another, even as I have loved you, that you also love one another. By this all men will know that you are My disciples, if you have love for one another" (13:34–35). Additionally, VanderZee states, "As a covenant meal, the Lord's Supper has the character of a pledge, an absolute commitment on God's part . . . the believing community dedicates itself anew to the service of God."[5]

Apostolic Application

Ten days after Christ ascended bodily into His Father's kingdom, the full weight of the new covenant was released and realized in the outpouring of the Holy Spirit, as thousands responded in both repentance and baptism. Luke, in Acts 2:42, documents that these new followers immediately incorporated the covenant meal into their gatherings, recording, "they were continually devoting themselves to the apostles' teaching and to fellowship, to the breaking of bread and to prayer." Additionally, Jude 12 tells us that agape feasts were taking place among the Christians. As the infant Church celebrated the new covenant meal, the New Testament writers employed four different terms to refer to the feast, according to its context. They are:

- **Breaking of bread** (Acts 2:42), indicating the presence of Christ.
- **The Lord's Supper** (1 Cor. 11), remembering the death of Christ.
- **Communion** (1 Cor. 10:16), suggesting a union with both Christ and others.
- **Eucharist** (1 Cor. 14:16); the Greek equivalent of the Hebrew *berakah* (the blessing prayer), indicating thanksgiving for the Christ event.

When the new sect began to grow exponentially, new problems arose having to do with the covenant meal, and a new Apostle was ordained to deal with these problems. In the process, the covenant meal got interpreted for the expanding Church. The apostle Paul continued Christ's sacrificial tone when speaking of the covenant meal. For example, in dealing with latent immorality in the Corinthian Church, he appealed to both the new covenant meal and the Passover meal in his exhortation. In 1 Corinthians 5:7 he wrote "Clean out the old leaven so that you may be a new lump, just as you are *in fact* unleavened. For Christ our Passover also has been sacrificed." He referenced the use of unleavened bread in the covenant meal to remind the Church at Corinth of their new life, purchased by the sacrifice of Christ, the Passover Lamb. In this usage, leaven represents the blatant immorality mentioned in the prior verse. Continuing in verse 8, Paul says, "Therefore let us celebrate the feast, not with old leaven, nor with the leaven of malice and wickedness, but with the unleavened bread of sincerity and truth." Paul exhorts the Church to be in the process of living out their new lives as they partake of the covenant meal, perhaps seeing obedience as the people's role in the covenant.

The behavior at this time in the Corinthian Church is an historic parallel to the Children of Israel. In Exodus 24 the Jews had been released from bondage and had entered into covenant with the Living God. Yet, because Moses took a while to get the instructions for their worship (40 days) the people grew impatient and fell into both idolatry and immorality (Ex. 32). In the Apostle Paul's next allusion to the covenant meal, he references the Israelites' behavior. 1 Corinthians 10:6–11 says:

> 6 Now these things happened as examples for us, so that we would not crave evil things as they also craved. 7 Do not be idolaters, as some of them were; as it is written, "THE PEOPLE SAT DOWN TO EAT AND DRINK, AND STOOD UP TO PLAY." 8 Nor let us act immorally, as some of them did, and twenty-three thousand fell in one day. 9 Nor let us try the Lord, as some of them did, and were destroyed by the serpents. 10 Nor grumble, as some of them did, and were destroyed by the destroyer. 11 Now these things happened to them as an example, and they were written for our instruction, upon whom the ends of the ages have come.

Paul exhorts the Corinthian Church to flee from idolatry on the basis of the covenant meal. He interprets it both as a **participation** in the body and blood of Christ, and as a **sign of their unity**. In 1 Corinthians 10:14–17 he states:

> **10:14** Therefore, my beloved, flee from idolatry. **15** I speak as to wise men; you judge what I say. **16** Is not the cup of blessing which we bless a sharing in the blood of Christ? Is not the bread which we break a sharing in the body of Christ? **17** Since there is one bread, we who are many are one body; for we all partake of the one bread.

Paul chastises the Corinthian church not only for their **idolatry** and **immorality**, but also for their **division** at this covenant table.

> For, in the first place, when you come together as a church, I hear that divisions exist among you; and in part I believe it. **19** For there must also be factions among you, so that those who are approved may become evident among you. **20** Therefore when you meet together, it is not to eat the Lord's Supper, **21** for in your eating each one takes his own supper first; and one is hungry and another is drunk. **22** What! Do you not have houses in which to eat and drink? Or do you despise the church of God and shame those who have nothing? (**1 Cor. 11:18**)

The Corinthians' failure was that they were not saving food from the Agape feast for those who arrived later (presumably those who were servants or slaves). Additionally, it appeared that they were making distinctions between various classes of people. While they may have used the bread and wine and said the right words to remember Christ's act of deliverance, they had completely neglected the larger covenant stipulation to "wash one another's feet."

It is in the wake of this church's disunity that Paul gives a new set of instructions for the new-covenant meal. He says:

> For I received from the Lord that which I also delivered to you, that the Lord Jesus on the night in which He was betrayed took bread; and when He had given thanks, He broke it and said, "This is My body, which is for you; do this in remembrance of Me." In the same way *He took* the cup also after supper, saying, "This cup is the new covenant in My blood; do this, as often as you drink *it*, in remembrance of Me. For as often as you eat this bread and drink the cup, you proclaim the Lord's death until He comes" (11:23–26).

This passage impels the follower to full-orbed participation in the covenant meal. The eating of the covenant meal is done squarely in the **present**; while at the same time it was to be a sign remembering and reenacting the **past** act of deliverance. Finally, the eating is counted as a proclaiming of the past deliverance until the **future** return of the Covenant-Maker.

1 Adolf Adam, *The Liturgical Year,* (Collegeville, Minnesota: The Liturgical Press, 1981), 9.
2 Strong's *Hebrew and Chaldee Dictionary of the Old Testament,* H2146.
3 Ibid., H2708.
4 Strong's *Greek Dictionary of the New Testament,* G0364.
5 VanderZee, 155.

Chapter Twenty-Five

Communion Throughout History

The rite of Communion has undergone much transformation and interpretation; certainly more than has Baptism. While both rites were affected by shifts in piety and the development of Sacramental Theology, Communion has suffered the most amplification in both meaning and usage. This chapter will attempt to summarize the various developments and applications of Communion. Like the preceding chapters on Baptism, I will let the main thinkers from each age explain their beliefs in their own words whenever possible. Additionally, the prayers that were prayed as an introduction to the rite itself will be included. This introductory prayer is known as the "anaphora," and is helpful in offering an additional glimpse into what the Church believed itself to be doing. Noted historian James White believed that an historical understanding is comprehensive when a student can identify the anaphora of the various periods and traditions.[1]

Early Patristic

The earliest non-Biblical document, the *Didache*, seems to emphasize both the **communal** and **eschatological** nature of the covenant-meal.

> Chapter 9. The Eucharist. Now concerning the Eucharist, give thanks this way. First, concerning the cup:
>
> We thank thee, our Father, for the holy vine of David Thy servant, which You madest known to us through Jesus Thy Servant; to Thee be the glory forever.
>
> And concerning the broken bread:
> We thank Thee, our Father, for the life and knowledge which You madest known to us through Jesus Thy Servant; to Thee be the glory forever. Even as this broken bread was scattered over the hills, and was gathered together and became one, so let Thy Church be gathered together from the ends of the earth into Thy kingdom; for Thine is the glory and the power through Jesus Christ for ever.

> But let no one eat or drink of your Eucharist, unless they have been baptized into the name of the Lord; for concerning this also the Lord has said, "Give not that which is holy to the dogs."

Early Believers related the wine to the vine, symbolizing the connection between David and Jesus, and perhaps their own connection to Him as well. The bread also held symbolism. The wheat that was gathered to make the bread represented the final gathering of Believers into the Kingdom of God. The cost of participating in this special meal was baptism, which was their initiation into the fellowship.

In the 2nd century, Justin Martyr's (100–165) *First Apology* described the anaphora by saying,

> There is then brought to the president of the brethren bread and a cup of wine mixed with water; and he taking them, gives praise and glory to the Father of the universe, through the name of the Son and of the Holy Ghost, and offers thanks at considerable length for our being counted worthy to receive these things at His hands. And when he has concluded the prayers and thanksgivings, all the people present express their assent by saying Amen.[2]

Two elements of his prayer are notable: the thanks and praise to the **Triune God,** and thanksgiving for being counted **worthy** to take communion. Additionally, Justin also linked Communion with the **incarnation** of Christ, offering this word of explanation:

> And this food is called among us the Eucharist . . . For not as common bread and common drink do we receive these; but in like manner as Jesus Christ our Saviour, **having been made flesh** by the Word of God, had both flesh and blood for our salvation, so likewise have we been taught that the food which is blessed by the prayer of His word, and from which our blood and flesh by transmutation are nourished, is the flesh and blood of that Jesus who was made flesh.[3]

Irenaeus (130–200) was a student of Polycarp, who was a student of John the Revelator. Irenaeus' main concern was to oppose the Gnostics, who were intent on separating the two natures of flesh and spirit. He appeals to the covenant meal in his argument by noting "For, as the bread that comes from the earth, when it receives the invocation of God is no longer ordinary bread but the Eucharist which comprises two elements, an earthly and a heavenly, so our **bodies which participate in the Eucharist are no longer corruptible**, since they now have the hope of resurrection."[4] Irenaeus worked forward from the two inseparable elements of the Eucharist to the two inseparable elements of Mankind: heavenly and earthly. The Gnostic separation of flesh and spirit were thus rebuked.

The *Apostolic Tradition* of Hippolytus records an anaphora that was probably used at the Church in Rome near the beginning of the 3rd century. Hippolytus mentions the creation, the incarnation and the redemption of Mankind in his opening prayer. He then prays the words of institution, finally going into a very telling explanation of what the Church thought they were doing. He prays:

> **Remembering** therefore his death and resurrection, **we offer** to you the bread and the cup, giving you thanks because you have held us worthy to stand before you and minister to you. And we ask that you would send your holy Spirit upon the offering of your holy Church; that, gathering her into one, you would grant to all who partake of the holy things to partake for the fullness of the holy Spirit for the strengthening of faith in truth . . .[5]

In using the words "Remembering . . . we offer," Hippolytus reveals a view of Communion as both a **memorial** and an **offering** back to God of the elements of the covenant meal.

Origen (c. 152–253) was a Platonist, meaning his Christian thinking was colored by Plato's notion of the world of ideas, of "ness." Plato taught, among other things, that physical objects were merely variations on an original, which existed in "heaven." Origen's analysis of Communion, therefore, emphasizes the spiritual nourishment of the Word over and above the physical action of partaking. He explains "It is not the material bread that profits the person who eats the bread of the Lord, and does so worthily: rather it is the word which is spoken over it."[6]

Late Patristic

The student of Christian history will know that a great many things changed at the dawn of the 4th century. A person would no longer be executed for being a Christian, since Constantine had legalized the religion in 313 A.D. Christianity spread quickly, and the Bishops of the regions became the new nobility. Author Donald Hustad notes that these Bishops "adopted the symbolism of the state which was now available to them because of their power and wealth: vast buildings and properties, lavish furnishings and vestments, and impressive pageantry."[7] Public worship became more formal, ornamented and priest-centered.

The various families of rites began to divide themselves into "East" and "West." The Doctrine of the Trinity was formulated and defended during this time, and it began to be incorporated into various rites of both liturgies. In the East, Basil the Great (d. 379) emphasized the single operation of the Trinity in the sacraments, and adjusted his anaphora accordingly. He also began to emphasize the "epiclesis," or, invocation of the Holy Spirit as the One Who transformed the elements of bread and wine into agents of communion with Christ. The *Apostolic Constitutions*, a late-4th century Syrian text, documents one such Eastern Eucharistic liturgy. The anaphora progressed as follows:

- Remembrance of creation
- Remembrance of the Old Covenant
- Sanctus
- Remembrance of the New Covenant
- Remembrance of the Last Supper
- A statement of offering in light of this remembrance
- Epiclesis

At this point, a summary of the Eastern Orthodox understanding can be put forth and then left, as this branch of the Christian Church has not changed significantly in the last 1500 years. Schmemann defines the Orthodox Church as any church that celebrates the Divine Liturgy. There are actually two liturgies (Basil and Chrysostom), and the chief difference is their anaphora. The Eastern idea of worship is always ascending into heaven's worship, rather than God joining their earthly worship. Schmemann says, "It is not 'grace' that comes down; it is the Church that enters into 'grace,' and grace means the new being, the Kingdom, the world to come."[8] Therefore, when the Orthodox Church speaks of the Eucharist, it is from a heavenly perspective. Schmemann explains: "Only in the Kingdom can we confess with St. Basil that this bread is in very truth the precious body of our Lord, this wine the precious blood of Christ. What is 'supernatural' here, in this world, is revealed as 'natural' there. And it is always in order to lead us 'there' and to make us what we are that the Church fulfills herself in liturgy."[9] Communion, in the Orthodox understanding, is inseparable from its context within the Divine Liturgy.

In the West, Ambrose (339–397) of Milan wrote that the bread and wine become the body and blood of Christ by the word of prayer. Leo I of Rome, in the 5th century, states during an Ascension Day sermon, "What was conspicuous in the Redeemer has passed over into the sacraments." Augustine, however, tends toward the symbolic or spiritual transformation of the bread and wine. He explains:

> My friends, these realities are called sacraments because in them one thing is seen, while another is grasped ... So now, if you want to understand the body of Christ, listen to the Apostle Paul speaking to the faithful: 'You are the body of Christ, member for member (I Cor. 12:27).' If you, therefore, are Christ's body and members, it is your own mystery that is placed on the Lord's table! ... When you hear 'The body of Christ'—you reply 'Amen.' Be a member of Christ's body, then, so that your Amen may ring true!

> Remember: bread doesn't come from a single grain but from many. When you received exorcism, you were ground. When you were baptized, you were leavened. When you received the fire of the Holy Spirit, you were baked. Be what you see: receive what you are.

These three Western thinkers seem to contradict one another, but "their fundamental interest is in the reality of participation in the body and blood of Christ in the Eucharist, rather than the transformation of the bread and wine."[10] Augustine used the word *Sacramentum* to unpack the way in which "things or actions could have the extra dimension of a sacred meaning."[11] He conceived of a two-fold link between the visible and the invisible, according to VanderZee. The first link was that the sacrament had to hold a likeness to what it signified. The second link was that the Sign had to be identified as a sign by a spoken word about it.[12] Because of his great influence, Augustine's overemphasis of the invisible over the visible sent his successors down the path of separating the physical from the spiritual. Thus, the **deity** of Christ overshadowed the **humanity** of Christ in their thinking. This, coupled with the previously mentioned priest-centered worship, eventually led to an inflated view and abuse of the authority of the Church.

Medieval

By the time of the Great Schism (1054) when Orthodox and Roman Catholicism officially separated, Western attention had shifted to questions about the transformation of the bread and wine. The Western (Catholic) Church had effectively divided Communion into two parts: the sacrifice (consecration and transubstantiation) and the Communion (the meal is distributed and eaten). Michael Welker summarizes the division: "Is Christ charging the Disciples to keep the shared celebration of the meal, or to consecrate bread and wine?"[13] He notes that if it is the later, then the priest performs the central event in Communion. This opened the way to the practice of **missa privata** (mass held for private devotion) and **missa solitaria** (priest alone), completely eliminating the community from Communion!

By the 11th century, the Fourth Lateran Council (1215) used the term "transubstantiation" to describe the change of the bread and wine into the actual body and blood of Christ. Originally, it is believed that this view was put forth to "combat the overly realistic view of the Eucharistic presence."[14] The Platonist thinking of Augustine, however, was not sufficient to explain this new understanding of transubstantiation, so Thomas Aquinas (1225–1274) employed Aristotelian philosophical categories. Aristotle divided all things into **substance** (a thing's essential reality), **accident** (that which is perceptible), and **matter**. According to Aquinas, in transubstantiation the **accidents** of the bread and wine do not change, but the **substance** is transformed into the body and blood of Christ. These philosophical nuances were difficult to put into common terms, and the original intent of counteracting an overly realistic view of the transaction was completely overshadowed by the thought of the actual presence of the body and blood of Christ.[15] This incredible mystery caused the table to morph into an altar of sacrifice, and it was subsequently moved farther away from the congregants. A second result was that people took communion less often, and there was great superstition that surrounded the consecrated elements. Instead of consuming the elements, some kept them, perhaps as a sort of good luck charm.

The Reformers

Some of the main abuses of the Roman Church had to do with the theology and administration of Communion. Communion had become a priestly function in which the congregation participated by observance, actually eating the meal only once per year. Rather than being a joyful action, it had become an additional sacrifice of Christ. Whereas the Early Church Fathers focused on what the covenant meal did for Believers, the Medieval church focused upon the transformation of the meal itself.

Luther (1483–1546) attacked the Mass as an additional sacrifice of Christ. He explained that "we do not offer Christ as a sacrifice, but that Christ offers us. And in this way it is permissible, yes, profitable, to call the mass a sacrifice; not on its own account, but because we offer ourselves as a sacrifice along with Christ."[16] He maintained the concept of the presence of Christ in the Eucharist through a concept called "Consubstantiation." This is the belief that the body and blood of Jesus Christ coexist in the consecrated elements with the natural elements of bread and wine. His formula of Christ's presence declared that Christ was present "under the bread, with the bread, in the bread."[17] With this concept, Luther took the first steps to counteract the superstitions associated with transubstantiation.

A colloquy was held between the various leaders of the Reformation in the year 1529, in Marburg, to discuss their mutual understandings on 15 separate issues. The one issue they could not agree upon was what happened at the Communion table. Luther's chief opposition was Zwingli (1484–1531), who thought the Reformation had not gone far enough. According to Zwingli, "the Lord's Supper was only the congregation confessing its faith in obedience to our Lord's command."[18] His views form the underpinnings to the view of Communion as an Ordinance, rather than a Sacrament.

The chief debate had to do with how to interpret the word "is," from Jesus' phrase "This *is* my body" (Matt. 26:26). While Luther took the phrase literally, Zwingli took it to mean, "This signifies my body." He contended that the elements memorialized the Christ event; that bread and wine were mere signifiers, rather than the work of God in the recipient's soul. Some consider this view to reflect the Enlightenment's separation of matter and spirit, while others regard this to be an appropriate application of Holy Spirit-inspired anamnesis (remembering through reenactment). Suffice it to say that good men do not agree.

John Calvin (1509–1564) took a mediating position between Luther and Zwingli by loosely aligning with both the Augustinian and Orthodox concept of Christ's presence. Though his intent was unity, both Luther and Zwingli rejected his view. Calvin took the phrase "This is my body" as a promise from God that He would be present, and considered "Communion as God's way of bending to our weakness"[19] Calvin insisted there was some form of real presence of Christ at the table, but unlike the Roman Catholic position, he did not try to explain what or how it happened. "How this is done, some may deduce more clearly than others. But be this as it may, on the one hand we must, to shut out all carnal fancies, raise our hearts on high to heaven, not thinking that our Lord Jesus Christ is so abased as to be enclosed under any corruptible elements. On the other hand, not to diminish the efficacy of the sacred mystery, we must hold that it is accomplished by the secret and miraculous virtue of God."[20] Calvin saw the Supper much the same as he saw the Word of God, and said the elements had no power apart from this Word. He explained in his *Institutes of Christian Religion*, 4. 17.

> "... the Lord also intended the Supper to be a kind of exhortation for us, which can more forcefully than any other means quicken and inspire us both to purity and holiness of life, and to love, peace, and concord. For the Lord so communicates his body to us there that he is made completely one with us and we with him. Now, since he has only one body, of which he makes us all partakers, it is necessary that all of us also be made one body by such participation."

> "... the right administering of the Sacrament cannot stand apart from the Word. For whatever benefit may come to us from the Supper requires the Word...."

> "... the sacraments have the same office as the Word of God: to offer and set forth Christ to us, and in him the treasures of heavenly grace..."

In England, the Reformation was embodied in the Anglican Church, with Archbishop Cranmer (1489–1556) taking leadership of the Church after King Henry's death in 1547. His main tool of reform was *The Book of Common Prayer*, which he published in 1549. The title indicates that worship was to be communal, rather than a performance of the priest. He retained much of the Roman rite, but changed the Eucharistic language to reflect the reforms of the time. References to transubstantiation were omitted, and the sacrifice was of "praise and thanksgiving" rather than of the body and blood of Christ. The offertory was now the congregation, who offered themselves "as a reasonable, holy, and living sacrifice to God."

Summary and Conclusions

The spectrum of belief regarding the sacraments is wide and sometimes difficult to articulate. The Orthodox and Roman churches operate under *ex opere operato*, meaning that the Sacraments bestow grace apart from the presence or lack of faith on the part of the recipient. Luther insisted on the presence of Faith within the believer, while maintaining the concept of consubstantiation. Calvin took a mediating position by teaching the real presence of Christ at the table without explaining how it happens. Zwingli insisted the covenant meal to be a memorial feast and an act of obedience, which became the understanding of Ordinance Theology. As with baptism, Quakers and Salvationists do not observe communion, believing these actions to be spiritual rather than physical. The differences between the various Communion traditions depend heavily upon the cultural perspective taken by each. The lens of culture and context through which each perspective peers dramatically affects their sacramental understandings.

Though steeped in an ordinance understanding of baptism and communion, this author was deeply intrigued by Calvin's view of the "Real Presence" of Christ in the sacraments, and anticipated converting to this perspective. I remain, however, not persuaded that God has **promised** to act during the sacraments. My questions regarding the efficacy of the Sacred Actions remain. It is not "do the sacraments do something?" but "*must* they do something?" I, personally, am convinced of the "Ordinance" point of view, and emphasize a full-bodied celebration of *anamnesis* and *prolepsis* as I lead and participate in Communion. I am what might be termed a Sacramentalist, in that I believe God often pours out a sense of his grace through his Creation. I have a deep and consistent devotional life, and present myself daily at the intersection of time and eternity, hoping to drink from the river of life. Sometimes I "taste" the water, sometimes I "swim" in it, and sometimes I just know it is there. As with baptism and communion, these experiences are unpredictable, and are always subject to the Sovereignty and grace of God. The student of worship should never presume that God will be predictable, except to be faithful to His own nature.

1. James F. White, *Christian Worship in North America, A Retrospective: 1955–1995.* Collegeville, Minnesota: The Liturgical Press, 1997, 314.
2. Justin Martyr, *The First Apology,* Chapter LXV.
3. Ibid., Chapter LXVI.
4. Irenaeus, *Against the Heretics,* 5.2.3. quoted in VanderZee, 4.
5. Robert Webber (ed), *Twenty Centuries of Christian Worship: The Complete Library of Christian Worship, Vol. 2* (Peabody Massachusetts: Hendrickson Publishers, Inc., 1994), 151.
6. Origen's *Commentary on Matthew 11:14,* quoted in Leonard J VanderZee, Christ, Baptism and the Lord's Supper (Downers Grove, Illinois: IVP, 2004), 165.
7. Donald P. Hustad, *Jubilate II: Church Music in Worship and Renewal* (Carol Stream, IL: Hope Publishing Co., 1993), 165.
8. Alexander Schmemann, *For the Life of the World: Sacraments and Orthodoxy* (Crestwood, NY: St. Vladimir's Seminary Press, 1973), 31.
9. Ibid., 43.
10. Lester Ruth, Lecture on the sacraments during class 701 at the Institute of Worship Studies, given in January, 2005.
11. VanderZee,166.
12. Ibid., 166.
13. Michael Welker, *What Happens in Holy Communion?* (Grand Rapids, MI: Eerdmans, 2000), 69.
14. Webber Vol. 6, 213.
15. Webber Vol. 6, 213.
16. Pfatteicher, 195. quoted from Martin Luther, *Treatise on the New Testament, that is the Holy Mass,* in *Luther's Works* 35:98.
17. *Formula of Concord,* Solid Declaration VII, in *The Book of Concord,* ed. Theodore G. Tappert, et al. (Philadelphia: Muhlenberg Press, 1959), 575. Quoted in Pfatteicher, 199.
18. Hustad, 191.
19. VanderZee, 137.
20. John Calvin "Short Treatise on the Holy Supper," 540. Quoted in VanderZee, 177.

IV

Towards An Understanding Of Sacred Time

Humans exist in time. We measure time. We give time. We mark time. We spend time. We waste time. We make time (we think). Rarely, however, do we stop to consider time. We keep track of birthdays, anniversaries and deaths. We celebrate notable days of the civic, academic and religious calendars. We anticipate future events that we plan or imagine will happen, all the while existing only in the present. But what is time and how might it influence corporate worship?

A Theology of Time

✤✤✤

A Summary of Christian Time-Keeping

✤✤✤

The Cycle of Life—Resurrection

✤✤✤

The Cycle of Light—Incarnation

An Introduction to Sacred Time

Why should a Worship Leader care to learn about Sacred Time? Because exploiting the power of the **CALENDAR** will become a tool to help your people live **in**, and live **out**, the rhythm and cycle of God's story. Biblically and historically, Christian worship has employed the calendar to revisit and reignite participation in this grand drama, but many modern Christians have set the practice aside in the name of autonomy or freedom from tradition. I hope to persuade you to consider some of the advantages "Sacred" time.

Stop for a moment
and wrestle with the following questions:

If God does not get tired, why did He rest on the seventh day?

If the Ten Commandments say to rest on Saturday (Sabbath)
why do Christians worship on Sunday?
Are Christians supposed to rest on Sunday?

What is the most important celebration in Christianity?

Does your Church's celebration reflect this importance?
Does your life reflect this importance?

What is the meaning of Lent? Advent?

Should Protestants keep these remembrances?

Chapter Twenty-Six

A Theology Of Time

Augustine speaks of Time in terms of memory (past), attention (present; also, "sight: or "attending to"), and expectation (future).[1] He mused over the ability of the mind to encompass past and present, even imagining the future, all outside the confines of actual time and space. He is said to have stated "whenever I imagine that I am in the present, it is already past to me."[2] Lawrence Stookey, professor and coauthor of *Handbook of the Christian Year*, adds that in some sense, "the present barely exists."[3] He continues, "The present cannot be conceived in isolation, as if it had a life of its own,"[4] and considers time a continuum, where the present is simply a moving edge between the past and the future. Ricoeur adds that "the mind itself [is] the fixed element ... [and] the important verb is no longer 'to pass' (*transire*) but 'to remain' (*manet*)."[5] Whatever time is, it is "interconnected with motion and change in the universe."[6]

Why, then, do Humans mark time? Early nomadic peoples chased the game and weather patterns, while agrarians planned for planting and harvest. Some of these ancient cultures based their calendars on the moon, while others looked to the sun to calculate a course of action. In each case, it seems that the measuring of time allows a People to measure and assess their progress. It enables them to participate and construct life, rather than merely watching it go by. Lastly, the measurement of time provides a lens through which to examine the patterns and principles at work in the universe.

A Theology of Time

The deliberation of natural patterns and principles of time necessarily introduces an investigation into a theology of time. An examination of this kind must shed light on both the past, revealing human worth, and on the future, revealing human hope. The fact that time and eternity have intersected and continue to do so is "grounded in the most basic of Christian affirmations ...

for our scriptures insist that in the days of the Emperor Augustus the eternal Word of God became flesh and dwelt among us."[7]

An abbreviated review of this Biblical convergence of time and eternity is in order. Genesis 1 reveals that time was created on day four, as well as time within time (i.e. it is measured). Day five documents life within time, while day seven is set apart as holy, with cessation from work as the demonstration of Sabbath's holiness. In John 1, time and eternity intersect as the Logos exists both out of time (v.1) and is made in time (v. 14). In John 17:5 we overhear Jesus pray to be glorified with the glory that he had before the world was made. Hebrews chapter 1 also reflects this concept, speaking of Jesus making purification for sins (a temporal act) before sitting down "at the right hand of the Majesty on high." 1 John 1:2 again reminds the reader that Jesus was "with the Father and was manifested to us."

The Development of "Event" Time

Because ancient cultures were oriented towards the seasons, early religions understood that life was cyclical. The Hebrew calendar, however, began to distinguish itself by marking *events* as well as agricultural patterns. Israel's aforementioned "holy convocations" were connected to either flocks or crops, and included Passover (which fused with the Feast of Unleavened Bread during the Exodus event), The Feast of Weeks (later called Pentecost) and the Feast of Huts. The additional feasts of Rosh Hashanah, Yom Kippur, Hanukkah and Purim were feasts that commemorated God's saving events.

It is interesting to examine certain New Testament events within the context of the pilgrimage feasts. Within the context of Passover, Jesus (age 12) talks with the teachers in the temple (Lk. 2:41 ff), cleanses the temple (Jn. 3:13–17) and endures his passion (Mt. 26:17 ff). During the Feast of Booths He taught and prophesied in the temple (Jn. 7:14–39). The Holy Spirit descends (Acts 2) and Paul hurries to Jerusalem (Acts 20:16) within the context of Pentecost.

The Christian calendar went even further in rejecting seasonal time in favor of time centered on the *Pascha* (death and resurrection) of Jesus Christ. New Testament time is not some "distinctive theory of time, but the fullness of time. What distinguishes it is its completeness, its *pleroma* . . . [it is] not some new philosophy of time, but a new quality of life."[8] Time, then, has a sense of completeness in God, while at the same time continuing on to its end.

Sacred Time

Time has no sacredness of its own, but rather, is a tool to be redeemed and employed by humans in order to participate and celebrate the eternal.

Sacred time, according to Patricia Wilson-Kastner, does three things. It connects Christians as members of the Body of Christ, draws the worshiping community into its broader union with Christ and with the World, and serves to focus Christians on the great feasts of the life, death and resurrection of Christ.[9]

Robert Webber, author of *Ancient-Future Time*, adds that the events of Christianity communicate time in the following ways: The incarnation presents time as **fulfilled time** (Mark 1:15; Acts 2:14–36), while the crucifixion epitomizes the **time of salvation** (Romans 5:6; Matthew 26:18; John 7:6; Colossians 2:15; II Corinthians 6:2). The resurrection, ascension and second coming of Christ all impart **anticipatory time**. (I Timothy 6:14; John 5:28–30; I Corinthians 4:5; I Peter 4:17; Revelation 11:18).[10] For the Christian, time is "the measure of purposeful life . . . [and] Liturgy is the medium for such expression."[11]

Because of the conflict between sacred time and secular time, Christians must have a correct theology of time in order to redeem it. Andrew Hill presents a summary of redeemed time as follows:[12]

-Time is God's time (Job 12:10; 33:4)
-Time is a divine gift, an act of grace (Ps. 139)
-Time is cyclical in the Bible (Eccl. 3)
-Time is linear in the Bible (Dan. 9:24–27)
-Time has purpose and meaning (Zeph. 1; Matt. 24)
-Time is short (Ps. 90)
-Time is for rejoicing (Ps. 124)
-Time is for praising God (Ps. 119:175)

A Vocabulary of Time

The vocabulary of a language often reveals what is valuable to the people who speak that language. For example, our thinking about "time" is necessarily limited by the English vocabulary of "time." Therefore, the study of time, and specifically liturgical time, demands a broader vocabulary than English affords. The following terms will be useful in understanding and describing concepts related to sacred time.

-**Chronos**: This is "clock" time, where we get our word "chronology." It speaks of time in sequence.

- **Kairos**: This speaks of an event in time, a specific moment, or even a crisis.

- **Anamnesis**: Literally, a drawing near of memory. Stookey says that this "does not imply a *mental* process, but a *ritual* process . . . remembrance by doing rather than by cogitation."[13] Zimmerman says that it is "not mere recall, but a remembering action, which is the present of the past."[14] It is in this sense, for example, that the Jewish Passover is both memorialized and experienced again in the enactment of the Seder.

- **Prolepsis**: Literally, to take beforehand. It is "the bringing of God's future into our present."[15] We sometimes experience this through songs like "We Shall Behold Him" and "I Can Only Imagine."

- **Kenosis**: Literally, to make empty. This is the word used to describe Christ laying aside his nature in Philippians 2:6–9. The great humiliation of Christ implies the great dignity of his divine nature, and the intersection of time and eternity.

- **Incarnation**: Literally, in meat, or in flesh. This is an obvious intersection of time and eternity. John F. Baldovin says that the fact of the incarnation and redemption of Christ "implies an irreducible tension between the already and the not-yet in the Christian experience of the world."[16] The pre-existent One embedding Himself into time is this word's relation to other time-words.

- **Resurrection** (anastasis): Literally "the standing up again." It is yet another concrete instance of the eternal dimension at work in our midst. The resurrection is not so much resuscitation as it is restoration to Christ's former existence. It is the center of both the weekly (Sunday) and yearly (Easter) cycles. The resurrection represents a "kairos" moment which took place in an exact "chronos" day.

These terms help us consider how an individual or a Body of believers can maintain a vital relationship with God, Who exists out of time. Joyce Zimmerman states the challenge in this way: "How do we participate in a historical event that is past and not yet come?" and "How do we *live* this mystery today?"[17] The observance of the Christian or liturgical year provides opportunities to live in this intersection between time and eternity.

1 Joyce Ann Zimmerman, "Paschal Mystery—Whose Mystery? A Post-Critical Methodological Reinterpretation", *Primary Sources of Liturgical Theology* (Collegeville, Minnesota: The Liturgical Press, 2000), 305.

2 Patricia Wilson-Kastner, *Sacred Drama, A Spirituality of Christian Liturgy* (Minneapolis, MN: Fortress Press, 1999), 33, Special Collections, *A Course Reader, Part 1* (Institute of Worship Studies, Florida Campus, 2006), 12.

3 Lawrence Hull Stookey, *Calendar: Christ's Time for the Church* (Nashville: Abingdon Press, 1996), 20.

4 Ibid.

5 Paul Ricoeur, *Time and Narrative,* trans. Kathleen McLaughlin and David Pellaurer (Chicago and London: The Univ. of Chicago Press, 1984,1985, 1988): Vol. 1, 18, quoted in Zimmerman, "Paschal Mystery", *Primary Sources,* 307.

6 Wilson-Kastner, Sacred Drama, *A Spirituality of Christian Liturgy,* 34.

7 Stookey, *Calendar,* 17.

8 Robert F. Taft, "The Liturgical Year: Studies, Prospects, Reflections", *Between Memory and Hope, Readings on the Liturgical Year,* Maxwell E. Johnson, ed. (Collegeville, Minnesota: The Liturgical Press, 2000), 14.

9 Wilson-Kastner, Sacred Drama, *A Spirituality of Christian Liturgy,* 39.

10 Robert E. Webber, *Rediscovering the Christian Feasts* (Peabody, Massachusetts: Hendrickson Publishers, Inc., 1998), 3.

11 Wilson-Kastner, *Sacred Drama, A Spirituality of Christian Liturgy,* 40.

12 Dr. Andrew Hill, from lecture notes in class DWS701 at the Institute of Worship Studies, Florida Campus, January, 2005.

13 Stookey, *Calendar,* 29.

14 Zimmerman, "Paschal Mystery", *Primary Sources,* 307.

15 Stookey, *Calendar,* 32.

16 John F. Baldovin, "The Liturgical Year: Calendar for a Just Community", *Between Memory and Hope, Readings on the Liturgical Year,* Maxwell E. Johnson, ed. (Collegeville, Minnesota: The Liturgical Press, 2000), 434.

17 Zimmerman, "Paschal Mystery", *Primary Sources,* 304.

Chapter Twenty-Seven

A Summary Of Christian Time-Keeping

The Liturgical Year, also known as the Christian Year, proceeds from the conviction that God is Creator of all that is, including time. This application of Sacred Time reveals itself in the development of the Liturgical Week, Day and Year.

THE WEEK

The Importance of Sunday

The Week is a primary element of the liturgical year, and is demarcated by the Sunday observance. While Wednesday and Friday were incorporated by the early Church as fast days (a break from Judaism, where Monday and Thursday were fast days), Sunday is the oldest element of the Christian calendar, and is central to both the weekly and yearly cycles. Because of its relation to the resurrection, it trumps all other celebrations and seasons. Mark Searle notes that Sunday is "the nucleus around and out of which the feasts and seasons of the year have evolved, and still it retains in itself the kernel of the whole Christian mystery . . . it encapsulates the whole economy of salvation."[1] He notes that the centrality of Sunday worship affects the local church in a significant way, stating "it is the day when the local church comes to realize itself as Church when all the faithful are called to find themselves within the whole story of God."[2] In fact, historically, the Sunday celebration is so important that "both kneeling and fasting were forbidden on this day in the early Church, as they were thought incompatible with its joyful character as a foretaste of the kingdom of God."[3]

Searle asserts "Sunday is essentially a post-resurrection appearance of the Risen Christ in which he breathes his Spirit upon his disciples for the forgiveness of sins and for the life of the world. As such, it is the point at which all the central images of the Christian life converge."[4] Robert Webber adds that "historically, Sunday worship expresses three truths: it *remembers* God's saving action in history; it *experiences* God's renewing presence; and it *anticipates* the consummation of God's work in the new heavens and the new earth."[5] The Sunday gathering, then, is the venue in which anamnesis and prolepsis connect and interact.

The Development of Sunday

The New Testament writers also attest to the centrality of Sunday in the liturgical year. But how and why did these Jewish Christians transition from keeping the Jewish Sabbath (Saturday) to a gathering on Sunday? Adolph Adam, noted German Scholar, writes that Matthew, Mark, Luke and John all document Sunday, the first day of the Jewish week, as "the day of the Lord's resurrection"[6] (Mt. 28:1 ff; Mk. 16:1 ff; Lk. 24:1 ff; Jn. 20:1 ff). It is apparent that the early Christians gathered to eat together (Acts 20:7) and to contribute to the needs of others (I Cor. 16:1–2) on Sunday. Paul also implies that the central activity of the Christian gathering, participating in the Lord's Supper, occurred on Sunday (I Cor. 11). There is also extra-biblical reference to the Sunday gathering, found in a letter from Pliny the Younger (c. 112), governor of Bithynia, to Emperor Trajan. He states "On an appointed day, they had been accustomed to meet before daybreak, and to recite a hymn antiphonally to Christ, as to a god."[7] Adam states that this letter describes both an early Sunday morning liturgy and a Sunday evening meal, which later was abandoned "under the pressure, evidently of imperial decrees forbidding suspicious gatherings in the evening."[8]

The Meaning of Sunday

A brief review of the Jewish Sabbath is essential in understanding the development and meaning of Sunday to the early Church, and its centrality to the liturgical year. As we have seen in Genesis 1, God chose to cease from His work on the seventh day. In Moses' presentation of the Ten Commandments (Ex. 20:8–11), the explanation of the Sabbath day is linked to the work/rest pattern of creation, and is assigned stipulations in its observance, i.e. to keep it holy and to cease from work. Later, Moses attached an additional Sabbath stipulation in Deuteronomy 5:12–15, compelling the people to observe the Sabbath by remembering their deliverance from Egypt. Searle notes, "these two sets of images of the Sabbath link it with the creation story and the Exodus."[9]

Jesus is the first to initiate transition from the Sabbath by declaring Himself to be "Lord of the Sabbath" (Mt. 12:8). Searle believes that Christ was "neither purifying the Sabbath law nor destroying it. Rather, he seems to be proclaiming that the Sabbath represented a vision whose time had come."[10] The twin themes of "Rest" (Genesis) and "Liberation" (Exodus) were now positioned in Christ.

Sunday was not deemed to be intrinsically sacred, especially to "Gentile Christians who adhered to St. Paul's view of the Jewish law as no longer binding upon them ... they would have had no interest in keeping any day of the week as a Sabbath."[11] It was "observed because of its historical connection with Jesus' resurrection."[12] Additionally, since Sunday was the first day of the week, early Christians did not view it as a day to abstain from their work. They did, however, employ a bit of "theological inventiveness" to the *name* of the day on which they celebrated the resurrection of Jesus. Talley, professor and leading liturgist in the United States, says that John's testimony of "being in the Spirit on the Lord's day" (Rev. 1:10) has commonly been "identified with the Christian observance of the first day of the week, the day assigned to the *sun* in the planetary week, as the day of worship celebrating the resurrection of Christ."[13] Because Christ declared himself to be the Light of the world, *and* because he rose from the dead on that day, the early Church appropriated Malachi 4:2 to proof-text their new day of observance: "The sun of justice will rise with healing in its wings."

Other Names and Images of Sunday

The Sunday gathering went by a variety of titles. "The first day" obviously refers to the resurrection of Christ on the "first day of the week" (Mt. 28:1 ff; Mk. 16:1 ff; Lk. 24:1 ff; Jn. 20:1 ff). Also, because many encounters with the risen Christ took place on the first day of the week, there was an underlying hope of encounter with the returning Christ on that day. A second reference, "The Lord's Day," could be a word-play on the phrase "the day of the Lord" implying the judgment and final reign of Christ. A third reference to Sunday also had this eschatological dimension: the title "The Eighth Day" extends the Jewish idea of seven as a perfect number. The concept of an eighth day "obviously signified something greater still."[14]

THE DAY

A second segment of the Liturgical Year is simply known as The Day. Brief weekday services, known as "the Daily Office," took place both in the city and in the monasteries. The city's Daily Office, known as The Cathedral Office, was designed for the townspeople who would attend when going either to or from work. The Cathedral Office consisted of two services: Matins, held in the morning, and Evensong or Vespers, which was held in the evening. A typical Cathedral Vespers would include the following:

- Psalms 140, 141, 129, 116
- Incensation
- Entrance with thurible
- Introit prayer
- Hymn of light: Phos Hilaron
- Readings (set for particular feasts and days in Lent)
- Multiple intercessions

- Appropriate hymnody for the day
- Nunc dimittis
- Concluding prayers

In the West, the monastic communities developed a system of seven or eight offices to be said daily, in an attempt to apply the exhortation to "pray without ceasing" (1 Thess. 5:17). The Western Monastic Cycle of the Daily Office is as follows:

- *Vespers* (at the end of the working day)
- *Compline* (before bedtime)
- *Nocturns* or *Vigils* or *Matins* (during middle of the night)
- *Prime* (shortly thereafter)
- *Terce* (during the middle of the morning)
- *Sext* (at noon)
- *None* (during the middle of the afternoon)

A rhyme is useful to remember both the name and focus of each of the hours.

At Mattins bound, at Prime reviled,
    Condemned to death at Terce
Nailed to the cross at Sext
    At none his blessed side they pierce.
They take him down at vesper-tide
    In grave at compline lay
Who henceforth bids his Church observe
    Her sevenfold hours always.

A typical Monastic Vespers would include the following:

- Initial blessing and prayers
- Invitatory psalm 103
- 7 prayers said before the altar, silently, by the priest during psalm 103
- Great ektenia (an intercessory prayer)
- Psalmody

Brian Wren envisions the austere existence of monastic life, and writes "the six hours of prayer are spread between eight services of worship, the Divine Office, which punctuate the day. The members of this faith community will meet more often for worship than for meals, and spend more time at prayer than at agricultural labor."[15] The monastic life is sometimes idealized to our Western minds, but the days were long, and the services of prayer were relentless.

THE YEAR

The third segment of the Liturgical Year partitions the year itself into cycles. Andrew Hill writes "The Western church—Roman Catholic and Anglican—adopted a chronological scheme highlighting two cycles of time in the church year: Advent and Easter. The Eastern Church—Byzantine and Orthodox—divided the church year into three cycles of time: the Menaia, the Octoechos, and the Triodion and Pentekostarion."[16] This explanation draws from the perspective of the Western Church, and will focus on the cycles of Easter and Christmas.

The Christian Feasts

To understand the basic principle in the development of the Christian Year one must understand how these feasts refracted into more specific feasts and "spread over a period of time."[17] In the first Christian century, for example, the feast of Pentecost memorialized the passion, resurrection and ascension of Christ, as well as the giving of The Holy Spirit. In the third century, Epiphany became the second holistic feast, and included the birth, baptism and first miracle of Christ (or a combination thereof, depending on the region). At the same time, Pentecost (the Great 50 Days) had divided into *Pascha* and Pentecost. By the fourth century, Pentecost divided into the feasts of Ascension and Pentecost, while Pascha divided into Holy week and the Triduum. Epiphany divided into Christmas and Epiphany. By the fifth century the Liturgical or Christian Year has fully developed into the cycle of life (based upon Easter) and the cycle of light (based upon Christmas). The time not directly included in one of these two cycles is called Ordinary time, so named for the ordinals, or numbers assigned to each Sunday.

A third cycle, called Sanctoral, developed originally to celebrate those martyred for the Faith, but continued to grow until every day in the year was assigned. To help "clean up" the calendar, All Saints Day was adopted as a way to both consolidate and to celebrate the lives of believers who had died.

The development of Christian doctrine was a driving force in the evolution of the Christian year. The great festivals of the Church embody important doctrines that "celebrate in our present experience what has occurred or what we resolutely believe will happen."[18] And like the Jewish Passover observance, the great Christian feasts "recalled an event to transform life."[19] Robert Taft, who has written widely on liturgical understanding, expounds, saying, "liturgical feasts, therefore, have the same purpose as the Gospel: to present this new reality in *anamnesis* as a continual sign to us not of a past history, but of the present reality of our lives in Him."[20]

Benefits of Observing the Christian Year

Because the Christian Year presents events in sequence, it can be an effective medium for presenting the *whole* cosmic story of God, rather than just the preferred elements. One challenge Christians have faced, from the ascension to the present, is how to maintain a vital relationship with someone Whom you cannot see. The Christian Year bridges the gap between contemporary Believers and the historical events of Christianity. As a discipleship tool, it is an invaluable resource for presenting the unseen in a tangible and historic manner. The Christian Year is an important and effective way in which both communities and individuals experience the convergence of time and eternity.

Application to Worship

Observance of the Christian Year can shape both corporate worship and the individual worshiper. A worshiper's theology is shaped and formed as one navigates the tension between the Christian and secular calendar. This tension is not to be avoided, but rather embraced as a tool of discipleship. Observance of the Christian Year is something tangible, and helps to keep the mystery of Christ central to the worshiper's experience.

Additionally, the Liturgical Year shapes corporate worship by providing a pattern by which to celebrate the entire cosmic story. It assimilates the pattern of dying to self and living to Christ, and provides Biblical patterns and expressions for the Church's adoration of God. Robert Webber submits that the practice of the liturgical year directs corporate worship to celebrate Christ as it "tells and acts out the Christ event."[21]

As with any cycle or pattern, ritualism and boredom can replace enthusiasm. On the other hand, the possibility of spiritual growth and discipleship through the observance of Sacred Time can be worth the risk. Rather than a repeating and unending circle, the Liturgical Year should be viewed as an ascending spiral, lifting both worship and the worshiper to new understandings and expressions of the mystery of Christ.

---

1. Mark Searle, "Sunday: The Heart of the Liturgical Year", *Between Memory and Hope, Readings on the Liturgical Year,* Maxwell E. Johnson, ed. (Collegeville, Minnesota: The Liturgical Press, 2000), 59.
2. Ibid.
3. Paul Bradshaw, *Early Christian Worship* (Collegeville, Minnesota: The Liturgical Press, 1981), 77.
4. Searle, "Sunday: The Heart of the Liturgical Year", *Between Memory and Hope,* 76.
5. Robert E. Webber, *Ancient-Future Time,* (Grand Rapids, MI: Baker Books, 2004), 169
6. Adolf Adam, *The Liturgical Year,* (Collegeville, Minnesota: The Liturgical Press, 1981), 36.
7. James White, *Documents of Christian Worship: Descriptive and Interpretive Resources,* (Louisville: Westminster John Knox Press, 1992), 18.
8. Adam, *The Liturgical Year,* 37.
9. Searle, "Sunday: The Heart of the Liturgical Year", *Between Memory and Hope,* 62.
10. Searle, "Sunday: The Heart of the Liturgical Year", *Between Memory and Hope,* 63.
11. Bradshaw, *Early Christian Worship,* 75.
12. Wilson-Kastner, *Sacred Drama, A Spirituality of Christian Liturgy,* 35.
13. Thomas J. Talley, *The Origins of the Liturgical Year,* (Collegeville, Minnesota: The Liturgical Press, 1991), 13.
14. Bradshaw, *Early Christian Worship,* 77.
15. Brian Wren, *Praying Twice,* (Louisville: Westminster John Knox Press, 2000), 23.
16. Andrew Hill, *Enter His Courts with Praise!,* (Grand Rapids, MI: Baker Books, 1993), 93.
17. Dr. Lester Ruth, from lecture notes in class DWS701 at the Institute of Worship Studies, Florida Campus, and January, 2005.
18. Stookey, *Calendar,* 33.
16. Webber, *Ancient-Future Time,* 25.
20. Taft, "The Liturgical Year," *Between Memory and Hope,* 22.
21. Robert Webber, *Twenty Centuries of Christian Worship: The Complete Library of Christian Worship, Vol. 2,* (Peabody Massachusetts: Hendrickson Publishers, Inc., 1994), 371.

Chapter Twenty-Eight

The Cycle Of Life—Resurrection

THE GREAT FIFTY DAYS

The Jewish feast of the Passover sets the date for the Christian feast of Easter and the Cycle of Life. Since Passover is based on the lunar calendar, this cycle of feasts is considered "movable" in that it will not happen on the same date each year. The duration of Jewish feasts teaches that significant events require significant time, if they are to be rightly celebrated. Early Christians appropriated the Jewish festival of Pentecost, and originally regarded "the whole fifty-day period as a single festal period which focused on the unitary theme of Christ's passage through death to glory."[1] Stookey emphasizes that the explosive nature of the resurrection was "too vast to be contained within a celebration of one day."[2] It was considered a season of joyous celebration, liturgically characterized by "frequent alleluias and a prohibition against fasting and kneeling for prayer."[3]

Pascha

The term "Easter" is regrettable, as it does not specifically refer to the resurrection of Jesus. It may be a variation of "Eoster" the goddess of springtime, or a derivation of the word "East," referring to the *rising* of the *sun*. A more historical word is "*Pascha*," but even that term carries some confusion. *Pascha* is a transliteration of the Aramaic *Pesach*, derived from the Greek verb *Paschein*, meaning, "to suffer."[4] Paul Bradshaw, a distinguished liturgical scholar, insists that the "original focus of the celebration was not on the resurrection of Christ but rather on Christ, the Passover lamb, sacrificed."[5] Talley explains that "this shift from memorial of the death to celebration of the resurrection manifests a shift in the nuance of *Pascha* from its original association with the day of the passion to the Sunday observance that was, in every week, the day of the resurrection."[6]

Another interpretation of *Pascha* appeared near the end of the second century in Alexandria. Clement, and later Origen understood the word as "passage" rather than "passion," referring to the Hebrew's passage out of Egypt. This thought represented the tendency of the Alexandrian theologians to "allegorize the Christian mysteries."[7] This interpretation may well lend itself to the current concept of embedding oneself into the story of Christ. Many Churches use the Easter seasons as a journey into the deeper things of Christ.

Controversy

In the middle of the second century there arose a dispute on the appropriate time to celebrate the *Pasch*. These two views represent not just differing dates for celebration, but also different emphases. Most scholars agree that the actual date of the Passover and crucifixion was probably Friday, April 7, 30 AD (the 14th of the Jewish month of Nisan).[8] Since Sunday was already the occasion of the Church's weekly celebration of the resurrection, the early Church naturally celebrated the annual resurrection observance on Sunday as well. The Church at Rome, and most other local churches, opted for the Sunday following Passover.

The opposing notion, held largely in Asia Minor and Syria, is known as the "quartodecimen" (meaning fourteenth) viewpoint. The Jewish Passover feast was always held on the "14th of Nisan, i.e. the first day of the full moon in the first month of spring, no matter which day of the week this should turn out to be."[9] This viewpoint embraced both the great symbolism of Christ as the Passover Lamb (I Cor. 5:7), and the historical connection of the Jewish and Christian feasts. This position might have found fertile ground with the Judaizers (Jewish Christians) who would have been naturally attached to the tradition of Passover.

The significance of this controversy lies not in the eventual date of the *Paschal* feast, but in its emphasis. The Sunday feast naturally highlighted the resurrection of Jesus, rather than His sacrifice. Alternately, the quartodecimen viewpoint stressed the sacrifice of Christ over his resurrection. The controversy was finally settled when the first ecumenical Council of Nicaea (325) prescribed the first *Sunday* after the first full moon of spring as the day to celebrate the resurrection of Christ.

This, then, is Easter Sunday: the Church's celebration of the Risen Lord! It is the focus and center of both the Week and the Year. The *Pascal* mystery is celebrated properly through both *anamnesis* and *prolepsis*, and must not be celebrated as if it were an isolated event. Celebrants must encounter and engage the risen Savior as their own. Zimmerman reminds us that the "*Pascal* mystery in its very meaning has to do with *us* as well as with Jesus Christ.

Consequently, it is less accurate to speak of the relationship of liturgy *and* life and more accurate to say that liturgy *is* life (or Christian living)."[10]

Pentecost

Today, Pentecost is most often celebrated as a *day*, rather than a *season*. Originally, however, it was known as the "week of weeks," beginning on Easter Sunday and including the seven Sundays that follow. History has gradually assigned specific themes to the Sundays of Pentecost, which are as follows:

2nd Sunday = Thomas (absent when Christ appeared to the Disciples)
3rd Sunday = Meal (after the walk on the Emmaus road)
4th Sunday = Good Shepherd (emphasizing the divine care of Christ)
5th Sunday = I AM (emphasizing the deity of Christ)
6th Sunday = Love one another (emphasizing the new command of Christ)
7th Sunday = Ascension (Sunday after 40th day after resurrection)
8th Sunday = Pentecost (Sunday after 50th day after resurrection)

I will highlight and discuss two of the more prominent Sundays in more detail.

Ascension Sunday

The ascension of the risen Christ into heaven is a crucial element of the resurrection, and has come to be known as the day of "*Christus Victor*," the Victorious Christ. The Biblical accounts of the ascension (Lk. 24:50–53; Acts 1:1–11) present another junction of time and eternity, and signal the completed work of Christ. This event is a vital part of resurrection theology, but is sometimes ignored by the modern Church. Celebrating the ascension can give hope to those who are suffering, and is often an opportunity to highlight the persecuted. Though the event itself is inexplicable, Ascension Sunday is an opportunity to embrace, rather than to ignore, one of the great mysteries of the Christian Faith.

Pentecost Sunday

The eighth and final Sunday of the Cycle of Life is called Pentecost Sunday. Once known as the "Great Fifty Days," it now generally refers to the fiftieth day after Resurrection Sunday, when the Church celebrates its birth. What was inherited from the Jewish festal cycle as a harvest celebration had been revolutionized by an outpouring of the Holy Spirit unequaled in the history of the world, resulting in a great harvest of souls! The Biblical account is to be found in the second chapter of the book of Acts, and describes the event as "a noise like a violent rushing wind" (2:2) and describes "tongues as of fire distributing themselves" (2:3) on those gathered together. The event transfused and transformed the fearful Disciples into fearless Apostles.

"Pentecost," says Robert Webber, "plays a crucial role in salvation history."[11] He believes that "Pentecost results in a clearer and deeper understanding of Jesus."[12] Pentecost is most often associated with the birth of the Church. Though some contend that the birth happened at the resurrection, this event is clearly a new empowerment of the followers of Jesus. In Peter's Pentecost-day sermon, he employs a prophecy from the prophet Joel (2:28–32) to explain the extraordinary behavior the community was witnessing from those gathered. This "last days" reference adds an eschatological element to the already pregnant implications of this day. The modern celebration of Pentecost is an opportunity to remind the Church that they are to utilize this same Spirit as they live in the time between the outpouring of the Holy Spirit and the return of the Son of God.

LENT

Since the resurrection of Christ is so astounding that it originally took fifty days to comprehend and celebrate, one might ask, "how can one prepare for such an event?" The Christian Year's answer is the season of Lent. The term "Lent" means "The Fast," or "The Forty." The season it represents underwent great development throughout the first four centuries. Christians originally began a fast of preparation on the day of crucifixion, but "Christians in Egypt and Syria went even further and created six days of fasting from Monday until the end of the Saturday night vigil."[13] As time progressed, the fast was further extended to forty days, in imitation of Christ in the wilderness. It is important to note that "the Lenten fast meant that individuals took only a single daily meal; in accordance with ancient custom, this was eaten in the evening."[14] Concurrently, church leaders prescribed this same forty-day period as a time for converts to make their final preparation for baptism and entry into full status of the Church.

At one time in its development, Lent began on the sixth Sunday before Easter and lasted until Holy Thursday. It now lasts from Ash Wednesday to Holy Saturday. Though this equals 46 days, Sundays are not included, as they are always *feast* days, and never *fast* days. Like Eastertide, Lent has acquired themes for each of the Sundays that fall within the season, which Robert Webber says helps to order our spirituality and enable us to sustain our repentance.[15] The themes are as follows:

1st Sunday = The temptation of X
2nd Sunday = The Denial of sin

3rd Sunday = A call to repentance
4th Sunday = (Rose Sunday) Focus on the healing power of Christ
5th Sunday = (Palm) A foretaste of Easter

Lent is a time for self-examination. It is a time to discern whether anything has crept in during the last year that might undermine or derail one's fervor for God. Beyond simply "giving something up for Lent," this time of preparation calls for "a greater openness to the word of God, a great zeal in attending the liturgy and performing works of charity, and a conversion (cf. Mk. 1:15) in every area of life so as to obey the message of the gospel."[16]

The Great Triduum

Triduum stands for "The Three Great Days," and is a fourth-century development that concludes the season of Lent. It includes the services of Holy Thursday, Good Friday and the Easter Vigil on Silent Saturday, and reenacts the days leading up to the resurrection of Christ. Augustine referenced it as "the most holy triduum of the crucified, buried and risen Lord."[17] His words, in fact, outline the meaning of the three services of the *triduum*, as presented below.

Holy Thursday

Holy Thursday is also known as Maundy Thursday (from *Mandatum Novum*: "a new commandment" in Jn. 13:34). This is the day "Christ instituted the new commandment of love both by word and symbolic action."[18] Its service remembers and reenacts the events of the Thursday meal with the Disciples before the crucifixion of Christ (see Mt. 26:17–30; Mk. 14:12–26; Lk. 22:7–23). Above all, it is a "commemoration of the Last Supper of Jesus and the institution of the Eucharist, as well as of the washing of the feet."[19] Many churches actually host an agape meal and a foot-washing service on this night. Also, communion is sometimes accompanied by the tradition of stripping the altar/table. This action is a dramatic portrayal of the humiliation of Christ, who was to be stripped and whipped. It also conveys a visual contrast for the Good Friday service that follows. Two additional services have gained popularity on Holy Thursday. They include the Tenebrae service (darkness/gloom/shadows), which is a monastic liturgy using candles, and the modified Seder meal, which adapts the Jewish Passover meal to symbolically represent Christ.

Good Friday

The name "Good Friday" may be a distortion of the English phrase "God's Friday." In view of the death of Christ, however, Good Friday memorializes "a day when the powers of evil were put to flight and dethroned; it was indeed a good day."[20] It did not appear as a liturgical observance until late in the fourth century, with Easter now designated as the celebration of the resurrection. Bradshaw believes that it "seems to have begun at Jerusalem in connection with the sacred sites associated with the passion and resurrection, and spread from there to other parts of the East."[21] Most of our information about the observances in late fourth-century Jerusalem comes from the diary of a Spanish pilgrim named Egeria, who was very thorough in her documentation of these events.

Although a Good Friday liturgy was slow to develop, it was always a day of "mourning and fasting inspired by compassion (a 'grieving fast')."[22] Contemporary crucifixion services are observed in a variety of ways. Some sing or focus on the last words of Christ on the cross, while others utilize a liturgy called "the Stations of the Cross." If Good Friday is observed in place of Maundy Thursday, communion is taken. Additional observances include a three-hour devotion kept from Noon to Three PM (the time Jesus hung on the cross), while still others venerate the cross (using the cross as a symbol which communicates Christ).

Holy Saturday and the Easter Vigil

Holy Saturday was the day of Christ's repose in the tomb. There is no liturgy for this day because it was a day of grief-inspired fasting. After midnight, however, the Great Easter Vigil, consisting of four services, was kept, in celebration of the resurrection and in anticipation of His second coming. The first of the four services begins with the service of Light. Today, this service begins outside the church with the lighting of the Christ candle, accompanied by the words "may the light of Christ, rising in glory, dispel the darkness of your hearts and minds." The worshipers then process into the church. The second service is the Liturgy of the Word, which includes various readings that tell the cosmic story of salvation. The third service is a Celebration of Baptism, and is the most symbolically connected to the resurrection. Here the catechumens (converts to Christianity) end their final Lenten preparation, and are invited to participate in the final service of the Easter Vigil, Holy Communion. The Apostle Paul draws a compelling parallel for us between baptism and the resurrection in Romans 6:3–4: "Or do you not know that all of us who have been baptized into Christ Jesus have been baptized into His death? Therefore we have been buried with Him through baptism into death, so that as Christ was raised from the dead through the glory of the Father, so we too might walk in newness of life."

Palm Sunday

Palm Sunday, so named for the branches the people waved (assuming they were palm branches) to welcome Jesus into Jerusalem (Mt. 2:1–11; Mk. 11:1–11;

Lk. 19:29–40; Jn. 12:12–19), is celebrated on the Sunday before Easter. It is the only day in the earthly life of Jesus in which He was recognized and welcomed by the masses as the King that He is. Since the day belongs to Lent, it is also full of irony, as one considers how the shouts of "Hosanna" would turn into shouts of "crucify Him" in just five days. Palms, processions and readings endow this day with both celebration and preparation. If a particular congregation does not hold mid-holy-week services, the acknowledgement of this week's irony should be included on Palm Sunday as preparation for the coming resurrection celebration.

Ash Wednesday

Ash Wednesday, so called for the application of ashes on the believer's foreheads, is the opening of Lent. It conveys both the sign of death and the promise of resurrection, as the ashes are applied in the form of the cross, with the words "Remember, O mortal, that you are dust; and to dust you shall return." This author believes that it is healthy and good to remind people of their own mortality at least once a year. The Ash Wednesday service marks the beginning of Lent, as well as the beginning of final preparation for those who were to be baptized on Easter. In the twelfth century, the church began a tradition of burning the palms used on Palm Sunday to provide ashes for the following Ash Wednesday.

Transitional Sundays

The Liturgical Year provides transitions both into and out of the Cycle of Life. Transfiguration Sunday is usually the Sunday prior to Ash Wednesday, and remembers the events on the mount of transfiguration. The image of the glorified Christ leads us into this season of self-examination and preparation so that our celebration of the resurrection may be whole and complete. Trinity Sunday is usually the Sunday after Pentecost, and teaches that the recently departed and soon-to-return Christ is fully God, as is the recently celebrated Holy Spirit. This Sunday transitions the Church into the Cycle known as Ordinary time with a strong foundation of the Triune nature of God.

---

1 Adam, *The Liturgical Year,* 88.
2 Stookey, *Calendar,* 53.
3 Ibid.
4 Paul F. Bradshaw, "The Origins of Easter", *Between Memory and Hope,* 113.
5 Ibid., 112.
6 Talley, *The Origins of the Liturgical Year,* 11.
7 Bradshaw, "The Origins of Easter," *Between Memory and Hope,* 114.
8 Adam, *The Liturgical Year,* 60.
9 Adam, *The Liturgical Year,* 58.
10 Zimmerman, "Paschal Mystery", *Primary Sources,* 312.
11 Webber, *Ancient-Future Time,* 161.
12 Ibid.
13 Bradshaw, "The Origins of Easter," *Between Memory and Hope,* 116.
14 Adam, *The Liturgical Year,* 92.
15 Webber, *Ancient-Future Time,* 106 ff.
16 Ibid., 94.
17 Adam, *The Liturgical Year,* 64.
18 Webber, *Ancient-Future Time,* 127.
19 Adam, *The Liturgical Year,* 65.
20 Webber, *Ancient-Future Time,* 130.
21 Bradshaw, "The Origins of Easter," *Between Memory and Hope,* 118.
22 Adam, *The Liturgical Year,* 69.

Chapter Twenty-Nine

The Cycle Of Light—Incarnation

EPIPHANY

"Manifestation" is at the heart of the Cycle of Light. The term Epiphany means "manifestation or appearance," and is a stationary feast, since its placement is based upon the *solar* calendar. The Apostle Paul's uses of the term epiphany referred to both the *birth* of Christ (2 Tim. 1:9–10) and to the *second coming* of Christ (Titus 2:13; 2 Thess. 2:8). Therefore, this "feast" has always been garnished with an eschatological perspective, having a view toward the end times.

As has been seen, the Christian Year has an evolutionary history, and the Cycle of Light is no exception. The observance of Epiphany began early in the third century as a celebration of the *baptism* of Jesus, and is the oldest of the celebrations in this cycle. The feast is believed to have originated among the Gnostics, who regarded the descent of the Spirit upon Jesus at baptism as the real entry of the Son of God into the world. The feast began to be observed liturgically towards the end of the fourth century, and had already refracted into more specific observances. In the East, the birth of Christ and the visit of the Magi were observed on December 25, while the baptism and first miracle of Christ were observed on January 6. In the West, however, the nativity alone was celebrated on December 25, generally observing some combination of the visit of the Magi, the baptism of Jesus and the first miracle on January 6. Since there was little centralization of the Church at that time, local congregations began to "adopt various annual festivals that were already being observed in other places."[1]

The reason for the East choosing January 6 as the date to observe Epiphany is not clear. Talley argues that it was arrived at by computation. Early Christians in Asia Minor had traditionally observed April 6 as the date of the *crucifixion*, and had attached the *conception* of Christ to this date as well, thereby putting the birth of Christ on January 6. Bradshaw also weighs in, explaining that other theories include the possibility of a "widespread pagan festival involving some form of divine epiphany on this day, in spite of the lack of explicit witness to its existence . . . the Christian feast emerged as a counter-attraction to it."[2] Today, Epiphany is most often celebrated as a *day* rather than a *season*, and brings to an end of the Cycle of Light by "completing the rhythm of expectation and fulfillment that defines this period of time."[3]

NATIVITY

The same vague speculation must also be done with the placement of the Nativity on December 25. The fact is that no one knows when Christ was born. Two hypotheses have gained popularity, however, and I will briefly present them. The "Calculation hypothesis" computes the date from March 25, a date accepted in the West as both the passion (death) and the *conception* of Jesus. This date is calculated from the belief that John the Baptizer was conceived on the Autumnal equinox, and was born on the Summer solstice (although there is no proof). Based on this date, Christ would have been conceived on the spring equinox (when Elizabeth was 6 months pregnant, according to Lk. 1:26) and born on the Winter Solstice (December 25). This makes perfect sense to the third and fourth century mindset, that believed important and/or symbolic events always happen in conjunction with the natural world, especially the sun.

The second hypothesis is the "History of Religion" hypothesis put forth first, author Adolf Adam notes, by L. Duchesne. In this proposal, the nativity was set alongside the pre-existing Roman celebration of *Natale Solis Invicti* (return of the invincible sun—northern hemisphere) in order to "immunize Christians against the attraction of this pagan feast."[4] A parallel theory attributes Constantine with the establishment of the nativity celebration on this day of the sun, fueled as he was by his desire to unify the empire. This might explain the presence of Christmas at his old capital of Rome, but presents a doubt when one considers "the dual problem of Constantine's limited presence in Rome and the evident absence of the festival of December 25 from the ferial calendar of Constantine's new Christian capital during his lifetime."[5]

Then, as now, the implications of the incarnation were central to the celebration of the Nativity. The incarnation is the grand convergence of Time and Eternity, described for us in 1 John 1:2: "the eternal life, which was with the Father and was manifested to us." Nativity commemorates "the appearing of the Eternal Word in our midst."[6] Christmas was originally a twelve-day feast, lasting from December 25 to January 5. Unfortunately, it became a season of much revelry, leading the Puritans of England to object to its observance. Once these Protestant Puritans came to America, they outlawed the celebration of

Christmas completely, considering it both idolatrous, and a leftover of Roman Catholicism (Christ's *mass*). It did not become a legal holiday in America until 1856.

The importance of the incarnation cannot be overstated. Leo, Bishop of Rome, saw Christmas as "not just a moving story but the starting point of our salvation."[7] God not only imputed eternal worth to Mankind by making him in His image, but He also elevated the significance of every human being by taking on human nature. The fact that God initiated a relationship with Mankind bids our attention to the amazing act of the incarnation. The Church's celebration of Christmas, therefore, must be far more than a birthday party for baby Jesus. It must present the history and the mystery of the Christ event described in the great *Kenosis* passage of Philippians 2:1–11, where Jesus divests himself of his glory and takes on human form.

ADVENT

Like the Cycle of Life, the Cycle of Light has a season of preparation that leads into it. Advent comes from the word *Adventus*, meaning "coming or arrival," and refers to the first visit of a new king or conqueror, or the enthronement of an emperor. The earliest mention of this feast is in 490 AD from Perpetuus of Tours, and references a 3-week fast. Initially, the time and length of Advent varied, but in 650 AD Gregory the Great established this season of preparation as consisting of the four Sundays before December 25. Contemporary Advent observances tend to focus more on telling the nativity story itself, but it has not always been so. Historically, the focus has been primarily on the second coming of Christ. Liturgically (and historically), the Sunday themes were as follows:

1st Sunday = Second coming
2nd Sunday = Judgment and Promise
3rd Sunday = Rejoice! Consider the One who is to come.
4th Sunday = The birth of the Promised One

Stookey says that Advent is a celebration of the "promise that Christ will bring an end to all that is contrary to the ways of God."[8] Since Advent is not a Biblically mandated season, Churches often feel free to adapt this season to their own culture and needs. Stookey offers one plea in this regard: "However it is achieved, worship during Advent should ever clearly and forcefully proclaim the fullness of the coming of Christ into our midst—future, past, and present."[9]

Transitional Sundays

The Liturgical Year provides transitional Sundays into and out of the Cycle of Light. Christ-the-King Sunday is usually observed on the last Sunday of Ordinary time, leading into Advent. Baptism Sunday is the Sunday after Epiphany, and is in keeping with the traditional celebration of the baptism of Christ on Epiphany (January 6).

Conclusion

Observing the Church Year can be both a challenge and a blessing. The obvious challenge is to avoid ritualism and legalism, while at the same time connecting contemporary congregations to the history and legacy of those who have gone before. Non-liturgical churches, especially, will benefit from observing the flow of the Christian Year. The Christmas and Easter cycles will give design and purpose to a generally haphazard approach to corporate worship, bringing preparation and meaning. The observation of days like Ascension Sunday, Ash Wednesday and Trinity Sunday will provide opportunity to teach and undergird some very important theology. The blessing of the Christian Year lies in the possibility of shaping both worship and the worshiper. The whole story of Christianity must be told, and told often, in order to live holy and authentic lives within the intersection of Time and Eternity.

---

1 Bradshaw, *Early Christian Worship,* 89.
2 Ibid.
3 Webber, *Ancient-Future Time,* 76.
4 Adam, *The Liturgical Year,* 122.
5 Thomas Talley, "Constantine and Christmas," *Between Memory and Hope,* 272.
6 Stookey, *Calendar,* 106.
7 Webber, *Ancient-Future Time,* 57.
8 Stookey, *Calendar,* 121.
9 Stookey, *Calendar,* 131.

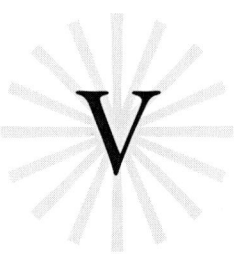

V

APPENDICES

1. Private Devotional Patterns and Plans
2. Worship Ministry Participant Qualifications
3. Scriptural, Historical and Theological Worship Designs
4. Worship Administration Websites
5. Event-Planning "Pert" Chart
6. Concert Promotional Plan
7. Sample Concert Press Release
8. Job Websites & Interview Questions
9. Ideas, Actions & Responses for Corporate Worship
10. Website Resources
11. Microphones: Design & Application
12. Projection Software—Overview and Comparison
13. Music & Worship Budget Considerations
14. Ensemble Concepts for Worship Singers & Bands
15. Personal Monitoring Systems
16. Evaluating a Worship Service
17. Vocalist Tryouts
18. Practical Advice for Worship Leaders
19. Resources from Sound & Light Publishing

APPENDIX 1

Private Devotional Patterns and Plans

Daily Routines
For a list of "How-To's" go to: http://roadmapsforworship.com/?page_id=511

1. A.C.T.S.
   Adoration; Confession; Thanksgiving; Supplication—(Philippians 4:6 loosely)

2. Temple Walk
   'Ulam (portico)—Thank God for the ordinary things in life.
   Hekal (main hall)—Praise God for specific things He has done.
   Debir (inner sanctuary)—Focus on the attributes of God.

Closely related—Thanks (I Thess. 5:18); Praise (Ps. 34); Worship (I Chron. 16:29)

4. Pray through the Great Commandment (Matt. 22:37)
   Love God; Love Others

5. "God Is" Statements
   Love (I Jn. 4:8)—Praise/Gratitude
   Fire (Heb. 12:29)—Confession
   Spirit (Jn. 4:24)—Worship/Adoration
   Light (I Jn. 1:5) Insight to the Word; Wisdom

6. Alphabet Adjectives
   Speak a fitting word of praise beginning with each letter of the alphabet.
   For examples of Alphabetical Attributes and Adjectives, go to:
   http://roadmapsforworship.com/?page_id=513

7. Review Scriptural Promises
   For examples of God's Resources, go to:
   http://roadmapsforworship.com/?page_id=515

8. Compare/Contrast—You are . . . I am . . .
   For a partial list of the Attributes of God, go to:
   http://roadmapsforworship.com/?page_id=509

9. Lord's Prayer
   Adore; His will; My needs; Forgiveness; Strength and deliverance; Praise.

10. Meditate on the Names of God
    For a partial list of the Names of God, go to:
    http://roadmapsforworship.com/?page_id=519

Reading Scripture

Book of Common Prayer—Daily Office Readings

Various Read-thru-the-Bible plans

Lectio Divina
- Read 6–10 verses; crawl into; bring senses and imagination
- Read second time; listen for a word or phrase that "shimmers"
- Read third time; Listen for what God says to you about that word or phrase.
- Read fourth time; rest in the story

Lectio Divina is an ancient spiritual practice from the Christian monastic tradition. Its title derives from the Latin words meaning reading and divine/holy. In Lectio Divina, we seek to experience the presence of God through reading and listening, meditation, prayer, and contemplation. Lectio Divina can be practiced both by individuals and in groups.

Lectio (reading the text: As you SLOWLY read, pay attention to what word, phrase, or idea catches your attention)

Meditatio (meditate on the text by placing yourself in the story. Use your imagination; what do you see, hear, feel. Then what? Consider what thoughts come to mind as you meditate. What are you reminded of in your life?) We can't really hear what the stories of the Bible are saying until we hear them as stories about ourselves.[1]

Oratio (praying the text: Now begin to speak to God. Tell God what word, phrase, or idea captured your attention and what came to mind as you meditated upon it. How is God using this word, phrase, or idea to bless and transform you? Tell God what you have been thinking and feeling as you've listened and meditated. Tell God how you hope this word, phrase, or idea will change your heart to be more like His).

Contemplatio (ask how you can live or apply the text? Or rather, what is my role in the Script?) "And then, Go and do likewise."–Jesus

We do violence to the biblical revelation when we use it for what we can get out of it or what we think will provide color and spice to our otherwise bland lives. That always results in a kind of decorator spirituality; God as enhancement. Christians are not interested in that; we are after something far bigger. When we submit our lives to what we read in Scripture, we find that we are not being led to see God in our stories but our stories in God's. God is the larger context and plot in which our stories find themselves.[2]

✣✣✣

Practice the Spiritual Disciplines

- Engaging Habits
    Study
    Worship
    Prayer
    Service
    Meditation

- Abstaining Habits
    Solitude/Silence
    Fasting
    Simplicity
    Chastity/Celibacy

Scripture for Meditation

Eph. 3:16–21
Phil 4:4–9
Col 3:12–17
Deut. 4:32–40
PSALM 116
I Jn. 1
I Jn. 3:1–3
Ps. 139:23–24
I Tim. 6:15b–16
Is 57:15
Rom. 11:33–36
Ps. 36:5–9
Ps. 73:23–26
Jonah 2:8
PSALM 99
PSALM 130
Ps. 36:9
Ps. 43:3–4

Scripture for Memorization—Topical Memory System published by the Navigators
http://www.navigators.org/us/resources/illustrations/items/Topical Memory System

LIVE THE NEW LIFE: Christ the Center 2 Corinthians 5:17, Galatians 2:20; Obedience to Christ Romans 12:1, John 14:21; The Word 2 Timothy 3:16, Joshua 1:8; Prayer John 15:7, Philippians 4:6,7; Fellowship Matthew 18:20, Hebrews 10:24,25; Witnessing Matthew 4:19, Romans 1:16.

PROCLAIM CHRIST: All Have Sinned Romans 3:23, Isaiah 53:6; Sin's Penalty Romans 6:23, Hebrews 9:27; Christ Paid the Penalty Romans 5:8, 1 Peter 3:18; Salvation is not by Works Ephesians 2:8,9, Titus 3:5; Must Receive Christ John 1:12, Revelation 3:20; Assurance of Salvation 1 John 5:13, John 5:24.

RELY ON GOD'S RESOURCES: His Spirit 1 Corinthians 3:16, 1 Corinthians 2:12; His Strength Isaiah 41:10, Philippians 4:13; His Faithfulness Lamentations 3:22,23, Numbers 23:19; His Peace Isaiah 26:3, 1 Peter 5:7; His Provision Romans 8:32, Philippians 4:19; His Help in Temptation Hebrews 2:18, Psalms 119:9,11.

BE CHRIST'S DISCIPLE: Put Christ First Matthew 6:33, Luke 9:23; Separate From the World 1 John 2:15,16, Romans 12:2; Be Steadfast 1 Corinthians 15:58, Hebrews 12:3; Serve Others Mark 10:45, 2 Corinthians 4:5; Give Generously Proverbs 3:9,10, 2 Corinthians 9:6,7; Develop World Vision Acts 1:8, Matthew 28:19,20.

GROW IN CHRISTLIKENESS: Love John 13:34,35, 1 John 3:18; Humility Philippians 2:3,4, 1 Peter 5:5,6; Purity Ephesians 5:3, 1 Peter 2:11; Honesty Leviticus 19:11, Acts 24:16; Faith Hebrews 11:6, Romans 4:20,21; Good Works Galatians 6:9,10, Matthew 5:16.

---

1 Buechner, Frederick. *The Seeing Heart*.
2 Peterson, Eugene. *Christ Plays in Ten Thousand Places,* 140.

APPENDIX 2

Worship Ministry Participant Qualifications

Worship Singers—Requirements

- Spiritual Maturity
    - Must have a seasoned relationship with Christ
    - Must be a daily worshiper
    - Must have a servant's attitude and heart
    - Must be a team player

- Musicianship
    - Good pitch; able to sing all styles; quick learner

- Lifestyle
    - Commitment to rehearsals
    - Good reputation within the church
    - Good reputation within the community

- Stage Presence
    - Must be poised
    - No distracting mannerisms

- Dress
    - No distracting dress

APPENDIX 3

Scriptural, Historical and Theological Worship Designs

BIBLICAL
- Acts 2:1
    - 1–3 God approaches
    - 14 Peter preaches (WoG)
    - 41 Baptized
- Acts 2:42
    - Gathering
    - Teaching
    - Fellowship
    - Table
    - Prayer

- I Cor. 11–14
    - Agape Meal
    - Table
    - Sharing of Spiritual Gifts

HISTORICAL
Didache and Justin Martyr
- Scripture Readings
- Sermon
- Prayers
- Table
- Thanksgiving
- Collection for the needy

Synagogue Pattern
- Praise
- Prayer
- Instruction

TWO-FOLD (WORSHIP & WORD)

Praise & Worship (Temple Sequence)
- Through the gates (Thanksgiving)
- Inner Courts (Praise)
- Holy of Holies (Solemn Worship)

Praise & Worship (Vinyard)
    Invitation
    Engagement
    Exaltation
    Adoration
    Intimacy Closing

Three-fold patterns

Revivalist
    "Preliminaries" (singing)
    Sermon
    Response (altar call)

Pentecostal
    "Preliminaries" (singing)
    Teaching
    Unleashing of spiritual Gifts

Theological
Four-fold patterns

Gathering
Service of the Word
Service of the Table
Dismissal

Gathering
Service of the Word
Thanksgiving
Dismissal

Four-Fold—Explained

Worship parallels God's Saving Deeds.
The order itself is the meta-narrative (the story)

- **Entrance** = God wants to be in relationship with us; draws me; invites me; COME!

- **Word** = God communicates with us by sending his Son; desires to restore relationship with us; provides a means of restoring this relationship thru X, the living Word; provides the written word as a testimony of his saving acts.

- **Table** = We respond to God's plan of salvation by saying yes; we accept God's reconciliation thru X; we take up our cross and follow him in discipleship.

- **Dismissal** = Becoming followers involves being sent; God intends for his people to be active as his representatives.

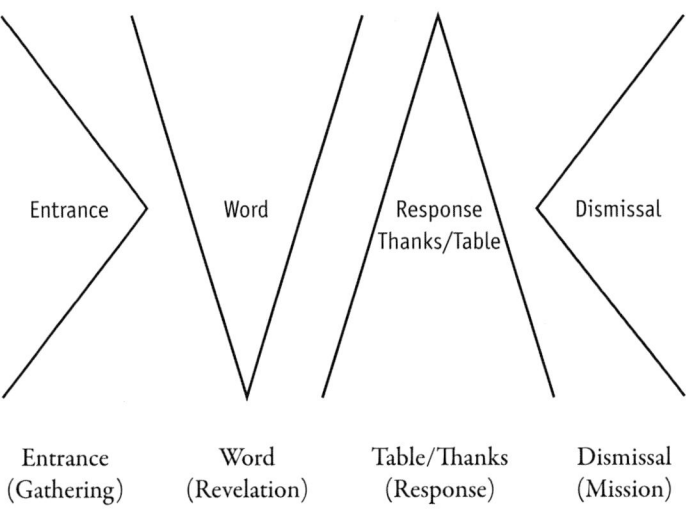

APPENDIX 4

Worship Administration Websites

Assembled by Frank Meeley

Introduction
Online Planning is a great way to get everything we do to consolidate all aspects of service planning and scheduling into one central place where everyone can access it. It is not only helpful for the Worship team, but it is useful for the entire church.

Vocabulary/Terms
Service Planning: The task of planning out the time spent and order of a service

Online Planning: The ability to do Service Planning on the Internet

Scheduling: The task of planning when which person is serving

Uploading: Placing things online so others can access them

Need & Usage: You can use online planning to schedule your team, distribute songs, allow them to listen to the songs, distribute a service order to those involved in the service as well as other areas of the church. This can also be used to upload media instead of transferring it by disk drive, email or CD/DVD.

Additional features
Blocking out dates for members
Media storage
Rehearsal ability with mp3's and Chord Charts
Replies from members
Automatic Reminders

Three Programs
CurrentWorshipplanning.com
    Easy to use, hard to navigate; not intuitive

Worshipteam.com
    Simple to use
    Price tailored
    Doc. Storage is too low
    Unlimited mp3 storage

Planningcenteronline.com
    User-friendly
    Templates
    Connectivity (email; iPhone; Facebook; etc)
    Warning; music must be streamable, so people won't download.

Comparisons
    - Worshipplanning.com
    - Worshipteam.com
    - Planningcenteronline.com

Expandability:
    - Worshipplanning.com: 50 planners, Unlimited helpers
    - Worshipteam.com: 500 People
    - Planningcenteronline.com: Unlimited

Learning curve:
    - Worshipplanning.com has a quick learning curve, but it's not very user friendly, meaning that the site is difficult to navigate.

    - Worshipteam.com is really nice from the preview videos, but without access to the site, it's difficult to tell.

    - Planningcenteronline.com is really easy to use as well as being easy to navigate.

APPENDIX 5

Event-Planning "Pert" Chart

Event Title: _____
Purpose: _____   Event Pert Sheet

Element	Supervisor	Sub-Categories	Sub-sub	Start	Confirm	Complete
Event Date		Event				
		Room(s)				
		Master Calendar				
Participants		Notify:				
		Directors/Performers				
			Choirs			
			Dance			
			Instrumentalists			
			Soloists			
			Drama			
			Choreography			
		Sound/Tech				
		Ushers				
		Janitors				
		Parking				
		Staff/Elders				
Peripherals		Parking				
		Bulletin	Printer			
		Promotion				
		Tickets				
		Content				
Preparation		Selection/Purchase	Music			
			Drama			
			Orchestration			
			Recording/Dup			
		Rehearsal schedule				
		Costume/Dress				
		Various Groups				

Element	Supervisor	Sub-Categories	Sub-sub	Start	Confirm	Complete
Rehearsals		Dress				
		Individual groups				
		Extra Weekend/Retreat				
Visual Media		Design				
		Develop				
		Additional Equipment??				
Decorate		Performance Room				
		Entries				
Scenary		Design				
		Build/paint				
		Install				
Aux Groups		Written/Recorded music				
		Extra Rehearsals				
		Kids = design off-time				
Choreography		Create				
		Teach				
Extra Musicians		Contact				
		Contract				
		Confirm				
		Dress				
		Payroll	Requirements			
		Music				
		Stand/lights				
		Other Equipment?				

APPENDIX 6

Sample Concert Press Release

One Month Before
- Advertise concert in church news letter.
- Invite local Bible Store to partner with church in any one of a variety of ways: financial; promotional; product sales; etc.

3 Weeks Before
- Free radio advertising. Do a search for radio stations; call appropriate radio stations, and ask to advertise on their free Community Bulletin board. Use "Radio Press-Release" provided. (Appendix 6b)
- Paid radio advertising, if budget allows. Target audience, and call station which reaches them. Pick the commercial package appropriate for your budget. Give them "Radio Press-Release" and a CD to make commercials.

2 Weeks Before
- Free Newspaper advertising. Call local newspaper and ask to have a blurb included in the religion section. Use "Newspaper Press-Release" provided.
- Paid Newspaper advertising, if budget allows. Call local newspaper and ask to place an ad in the calendar section. Use "Newspaper Press-Release" and photo, provided.
- Contact local churches. Invite their people to the concert, and ask them to put a blurb in their bulletin. Possibly send them a "Bulletin Master" provided.
- Hang posters around facility.
- Ask local Bible Bookstore to display a poster.

1 Week Before
- Place insert in church bulletin, using "Bulletin Master" provided.
- Send reminder memo to all groups within the church:
    - Choir/music groups
    - Adult Sunday School Classes
    - Home Bible Study Leaders

Day of Concert
- Show promotional video during offertory.

APPENDIX 7

Sample Concert Press Release

For Details, Contact: Artist Name
Jane Doe Address
1.800.555-5555 Address
www.xxxxxx.com Email: xxxxxx

ARTIST NAME news release

Accomplished! Humorous! Worshipful! Versatile!

Describe the exceptional talent of _____

This exciting California duo creates a spirit that is contagious!

Attention music lovers!

Artist Name will be performing on _____ at the

DATE

_____church

NAME OF CHURCH

Artist Name
- Performs an amazing combination of sacred music, classical stylings and hip rhythms.
- Concerts are worshipful, entertaining and humorous.
- Audiences enjoy a delightful variety of instruments and styles, including piano, piccolo trumpet, violin, mandolin, flute and guitar.

Don't miss this opportunity to hear **Artist Name**
in concert, beginning at _____ p.m.

TIME

on _____

DATE

sponsored by the_____ church

NAME OF CHURCH

For more information, call _____ for directions or more information

PHONE NUMBER

For Immediate Release

APPENDIX 8

Job Websites & Interview Questions

Assembled by Drew Walsh, Randall Goulard,
Frank Meeley, Michael Mikasa, Josh Park

Following the questions below are an additional list of questions that various people have been asked during actual job interviews. Don't try to write answers to every question, but do have a general idea as to how you would speak to the points. Preparation is the key to a good interview, but calling is the key to a successful ministry.

Job Websites

http://www.creatormagazine.com/dnn/CreatorLeadershipNetwork/PositionListings/tabid/381/Default.aspx

http://www.christianitytoday.com/career/

http://www.churchstaffing.com/JobSeeker/JobSearch.aspx,

http://www.worshipleader.com/jobboard

Questions to Ask a Church, Pastor or Search Committee.
- How would you describe our future relationship, under the best conditions?
- Who are/were your mentors?
- What is your favorite verse/book of the Bible?
- Why did the last person leave?
- What is your church's goal, mission statement and vision?
- What is your personal expectation of someone in this position?
- Describe the work environment.
- What are the non-negotiables of this position?
- What is your idea or picture of a great or successful worship service?
- Are there any preexisting biases or resentments to this position, no matter who is in it?
- What is the role/priority of worship in your church vision?
- What is your management style?
- What role does worship music play on Sunday, for example is it just a platform for sermons, is it the climax of the service?
- What is your definition of worship?
- Does the church take an official or unofficial stand in politics?
- Are there other leaders involved in the worship ministry?
- What would be my relationship with them?
- To whom do I report? What is the chain of command?
- What is the church polity?

- What is your theology on divorce?
- What are the services, fellowship meetings, retreats, etc. for which I will be responsible?
- If I am called to be a part of outside conferences and seminars, are these seen as extensions of this church ministry, or my personal ministry?
- What is the current state and stable of musicians, equipment, and technology?
- Worship pastors face a lot criticism. Will I receive your support and protection?
- What are the seasonal expectations, for example during Christmas or Easter?
- Would I have any other areas of responsibility?
- Is the church still in debt or paying off a mortgage?
- What are the time expectations?
- Does Sunday/weekend worship count as a workday?
- What are three things you are looking for in a church?
- Does your staff have an evaluation process? Weekly? Monthly? How often?
- Is there freedom in styles (musically, layout, etc) or do you have expectations of what you want?
- Chain of command?
- How do you feel about non-Christians on stage during worship?
- What is your definition of worship?
- What is the dress like?
- Would you ever pay for musicians?
- Are there seasonal expectations?
- Am I being paid to train musicians in the church?
- Would you be willing to pay for an online planning membership?
- Am I allowed to take opportunities outside the church to lead worship?
- Will this require me to take time off?
- Can I keep the money?
- Does the money go to the church?
- What are your weekly hour expectations?
- How do you feel about continued education?
- Training conferences?
- Worship conferences?—For resources, for refreshment, for training.
- Is there budget for conferences?
- Will you help pay for continued education?
- Does the church have budget for videos, music, other worship elements?
- How much of my time do you anticipate will be spent on rehearsing, pastoral care, pastoral meetings, administration work?
- Will there be pastoral care requirements?

✠✠✠

Questions a Church, Pastor or Search Committee may ask.
- How is your devotional life? How do you maintain your own relationship with Christ?
- What is your biggest weakness?
- What is your theological bent?
- Are you charismatic?
- What is your greatest asset?
- What is your salary expectation?
- Describe your work ethic?
- What are your spiritual gifts?
- Give your personal testimony.
- Why do you lead worship?
- What experience do you have in leading worship?
- What is your favorite style of worship?
- Who influences your worship style?
- Where are you on your spiritual Journey with God?
- How do you avoid sexual temptation with the opposite sex? Strategies?
- What is your view on women in ministry?
- What is your theological leaning?
- What is your stand on homosexuality?
- What do you think the worship pastor's job ought to be?
- Do you have any other passions/interests?
- How much would you expect to be paid?
- What makes you think you can do this job?
- What do you know about this particular position?
- What do you know about our church and its philosophy of ministry?
- What brings you to apply for this particular position?
- What is your philosophy regarding worship?
- What does worship mean to you?
- What do you feel would be your biggest challenge in doing ministry here?
- Can you give us an example of a time that you've experienced a truly worshipful moment?
- What is your belief about worship as a ministry to those involved?
- Can you give an example of a time that you resolved conflict?
- What are the other commitments in your life?
- How do you plan on meeting those and your responsibilities here?
- What has been your experience working with musical groups?
- What is your leadership style?
- Do you have a personal vision or mission statement?
- Do you set goals? What are they?

- What other ministry experience do you have: for example, parachurch, youth work, music ministries, etc?
- List "secular" work that has helped in preparation for your vocational ministry.
- Give a brief summary of your conversion experience.
- Can you agree with our Statement of Faith? Briefly describe points with which you may have reservations.
- Appraise yourself in the following functions of ministry, and briefly share your views on the topic: Leading worship for a congregation, Programming all elements of a service, Preparation and rehearsal of band and vocalists, Recruiting, training and equipping, Creativity, Leadership, Organizational abilities.
- Rank the above (question #6) ten functions of ministry listed in order of where you feel most competent/effective. (#1 being most competent and #7 least competent)
- Describe the style of music in which you prefer to lead a congregation. In what other styles do you consider yourself competent to lead others?
- Briefly describe the role evangelism has in your ministry and personal life?
- Describe your vision for worship in the local church and how you inspire others to catch that vision.
- List the types of administrative and management experiences you have had and evaluate your skills.
- Describe how you handle personality conflicts between yourself and others. Give examples.
- Do you play an instrument (s)? Please describe your proficiency on each and indicate whether you use the instrument in leading worship.
- Is there anything from your past that we should be aware (divorce, addictions, affairs, etc)? If so please explain.
- When you consider this position, what priorities for the job come to mind? What do you believe we should be looking for in an applicant?
- Explain and describe the core values of your ministry philosophy.
- What area(s) of ministry are you most passionate about? How do you think people develop a sense of "calling"?
- If you could pursue any avenue of ministry, and if money, time, and success were not issues to contend with, what would your dream be?
- What are your expectations and things you need most from the leaders of a church? from a church staff? from a supervisor?
- What are your top long-term goals? What do you see yourself doing 15 years from now?
- How would some people describe you as a leader? Why?
- What have been some of your greatest successes in ministry? What did you learn about yourself? About ministry?
- What has been your worst failure in ministry? Why did it not succeed? What did you learn?
- What are your top three spiritual gifts? What has led you to this conclusion?

- Speaking of spiritual gifts, explain your theological position on the baptism/filling of the Spirit and the validity of the "sign gifts" for the church today; i.e. (1 Corinthians 12:8–10)
- List two or three individuals in your life who have affirmed your ministry abilities and describe your relationship with each. May we contact them?
- Who are your best critics? Do you know why they are? What would they say about you? May we contact them?
- Tell us about your family background. What were some of your struggles growing up?
- How have you worked through any family struggles in your own life? What are your best memories?
- How does your immediate family (spouse, children) support or not support you in ministry? Tell us about your children. In what ways do you spend time with them? What do you do to lead them spiritually?
- Do you have any financial obligations? Any credit card debt? Educational debt? What are you paying off (if anything)?
- What level of income do you feel would be necessary for you to feel responsible towards your family and released into ministry?
- Authenticity and vulnerability are highly valued at our church. How do you define these two words and how have you incorporated them into your own personal lifestyle?
- Describe a conflict you have had with someone. What steps did you take to deal with that conflict?
- Who are the mentors in your life? May we contact them?
- Tell us about the areas of your life in which you feel most susceptible. In other words, if you were ever to "fall" and have to leave ministry, in what areas would it most likely be?
- What are you doing to protect yourself? Who are you accountable to?
- Pick out a day from last week and describe it in detail AM-PM. How do you relax?
- What priority does physical fitness have in your life?
- What are your key spiritual disciplines and how do you maintain authenticity and enthusiasm in your life in Christ? What are you reading in the Bible?
- What have been some answers to recent prayers?
- When was the last time you shared your faith?
- Who are 2 or 3 seekers you've built bridges with? How? What is the cutting edge of your spiritual life?
- What do you believe would be the unique contribution you could bring to the life of our church as a Worship Pastor?
- As a Worship Pastor, how would you describe your leadership and managerial style?

APPENDIX 9

Ideas, Actions & Responses for Corporate Worship

Gathering
- Sing gathering songs
- Group "Calls to Worship"
- Let the first words be about God
- "We gather in the name of the Father, Son, Holy Spirit"
- "Let us present ourselves to God as a lump of clay would to the Potter"
- See also Book of Common Prayer
- Use the Temple liturgies' (Ps. 93–100) traditional calls to worship (Ps. 95:1–2; Ps. 96:7–9)
- Is. 55:1–3
- Ps. 19:14

Announcements
- Always tie announcements to the purpose of the Church; i.e. "Because we as a Church are resolved to _____, we invite you to gather for _____."
- Be careful! Many Churches have two or three announcement times; they just don't call it that.

Intros to help people engage with the reading of the Word of God
- "I am about to open the faucet of God's Words to us. Drink some; cool yourself; wash your wounds. But please, don't just let it go down the drain."
- "I am about to uncork the finest of wines. Don't just drink it, and don't turn it down. Savor it; smell it; observe the complexities of it; relish it."
- "Don't just hear these words; listen to them. I invite you now, in the words of Jeremiah, to 'Stand at the crossroads, and see, and ask for the ancient paths,
  Where the good way is, and walk in it;
  And you will find rest for your souls.'"
- "Don't just hear the sound of the words. Listen; analyze; evaluate; interact."
- "I invite you now to come in from the fields of your lives. Take a long, cool drink of pure, cold water, drawn from the well of abundant life."
- "I am about to slice the Bread of Life before you. I invite you to devour it as you listen."
- "Listen to these words as though God, Himself, were saying these things to our Church."
- "I am about to read holy words to you. Be attentive, as God has sent these words from the place where light is born, to be penned and preserved for us to hear. Listen for God's voice. Try to hear the overtones of His heart between the words, for it will be my voice, but His message."

- "Give ear! God has breathed-out these words to faithful people who would write them down for us! As you listen, see if you can sense His presence; touch His hand; feel His breath."
- Read Ps. 119:47–48 and have people lift hands and meditate as the WoG is read.
- Have various groups read, while others listen (Men/Women; Old/Young; etc.)

Meditation
- Meditate on a short phrase of Scripture
- "Listen to Jeremiah's love for God's words. He said (recite Jer. 15:16); then say 'I invite you to eat these words as I read; to take them into yourselves, and to allow them to nourish you; to strengthen you; to infuse you with life.'"
- Think on the NT's "God Is" statements (Light; Fire; Love; Spirit)
- Results of Salvation
- Synonyms for salvation (adoption; mercy; forgiveness; grafting-in; etc.)
- Promises (reserve a place in heaven; never leave)
- Is. 55:6–9
- Jer. 2:13

Intros to Songs
- Whenever possible, tie to Scripture
- If a prayer song, say "Pray this together" then just start singing.

Greeting/Acknowledging/Edifying others
- Passing of peace (in place of "Meet & Greet")
- Tie it to corporate commands, i.e. "consider one another more important . . ." or "consider how to stimulate one another to love and good works . . ."
- Silent prayer for those next to or around you
- Hand on shoulder during prayer

Offering
- Whisper a word of thanks for the privilege of being involved with the KoG
- Whisper "take my heart"
- Whisper "I wish it were more"
- Walk forward to lay offering before God
- Sing songs of thanks while passing plate
- Speak Rom. 11:33–36

Praise Responses ("Why worship a God who did things in the past, but does nothing now?")
- Quietly raise/lower hand if God has: comforted; healed; provided; guided; etc.
- Speak out your thanks
- What has He done in you that you could not do in yourself? He has . . .
- How has He shown himself to be faithful? Trustworthy? Strong?

Worship Responses
Speak out God's:
- Names
- Attributes
- Deeds (You have . . .)

Prayer Responses
- Ps. 139—"May the words of my mouth . . ."
- Say benedictions (see "Benedictions")
- Pray audibly
- Say/sing/meditate through the "Lord's Prayer"
- How has God shown Himself to faithful this week? (He _____ me . . .)

Responses of Resolve
- Rom. 1:16
- Gal. 2:20
- Job 27:13
- Ps. 142:5
- Speak/Sing a Creed (Nicene; Apostles; Athanasius'; etc.)

Singing Responses
- Prayer songs
- Praise songs
- Read, then sing the Scripture

Congregational Prayer
- Is. 58:9
- Mix up how prayer is done (silently; corporate whisper; leader prompt; prompt with a slide)
- Confession
    Lead through five words of sin (sin; guile; transgress; trespass; iniquitous) and have people agree
    Leader prays, people sporadically agree with "me, too, Lord."
    Litany (Book of Common Prayer)
    Litanies: "I have sinned"
    Allow THS to put a finger on an area which is offensive to Him.
- Our World
    School closest to where you live
    Government officials
    Justice for the oppressed
- His Kingdom come
    Missionaries
    Countries
    Persecuted Church
    Other religions/cults

- Our needs
    - Guidance
    - Comfort
    - Provision
    - Healing
    - Salvation of fam/friends/neighbors

Postures
- Spread-out hands (low) during prayer
- Stand—always hook action to meaning! i.e. stand to honor; stand to identify; stand in the newness of life; etc.
- Bow (at waist; head; etc.)
- Stretch-out a hand for prayer (a la laying-on of hands)
- Hands: Palms up to receive; down to drop or lay-down; fist to hold-on tightly
- Lift hands corporately.

Good group-spoken benedictions
- Ps. 106:47–48
- Ps. 48:9–10
- Ps. 33:20–22
- Ps. 27 13–14
- 1 Tim. 6:15–16
- Rom. 11:33–36
- All speak the Gloria Patri
- In response to the priestly blessing (Num. 6:24–26), have the people answer with Ps. 67:1–7

Benedictions: say over people with heads bowed or palms open
- 1 Chron. 29:10–12
- Is. 58:6–11
- Heb. 13:20–21
- 1 Thess. 5:23–24
- Num. 6:24–26
- Eph. 3:16–21
- Rom. 15:13
- Sing "Parting/Mission" songs, i.e. "Let Love be Multiplied"

APPENDIX 10

Website Resources

Assembled by Drew Walsh, Randall Goulard, Frank Meeley, Michael Mikasa, Josh Park, Debbie Gin, Jim Altizer

Worship
1. Roadmaps For Worship (Tips & Resources for Worship Leadership): www.RoadmapsForWorship.com
2. Renovaré: http://www.renovare.org/
3. Jesuit online devotion: http://sacredspace.ie/
4. Daily Lectionary (ESV): http://www.gnpcb.org/esv/devotions/bcp/

Online Planning Tools
1. www.Worshipplanning.com
2. www.Worshipteam.com
3. www.Planningcenteronline.com

Music and Charts
1. www.CCLI.com
2. www.PraiseCharts.com
3. www.angelmusicusa.com
4. www.sheetmusicdirect.us
5. www.HigherPraise.con
6. www.1Christian.net

Audio Gear
1. www.sweetwater.com
2. www.musiciansfriend.com
3. www.guitarcenter.com
4. www.bhproaudio.com
5. www.shure.com
6. www.sennheiser.com
7. www.audio-technica.com
8. www.akg.com
9. www.neumannusa.com
10. www.beyerdynamic-usa.com/en/home.html
11. www.dpamicrophones.com/
12. www.mercenary.com

Bible Web Sites
1. Bible Basics: http://netministries.org/bbasics/bbasics.html
2. Bible Phrases: http://www.phrases.org.uk/meanings/bible-phrases-sayings.html
3. International Bible Society: http://www.ibs.org

4. Sacred Scripture: http://www.shc.edu/theolibrary/bible.htm (links to multiple Bible sites)
5. Bible Gateway: http://www.biblegateway.com/
http://bible.gospelcom.net (various English and other language translations)
6. Bible Study Tools: http://bible.crosswalk.com (has concordance, various English translations)
7. Five Gospel Parallels: http://www.utoronto.ca/religion/synopsis (hypertexted)
8. Online Translations of the Bible: http://rockhay.tripod.com/worship/translat.htm (collection of links to online Bibles)

Encyclopedias and Dictionaries
1. Hypertext Bible Dictionary: http://www.bible.gen.nz/dictionary.htm
2. Dictionary of American Hymnology: http://www.oberlin.edu/library/DAH.html (data on hymns and writers)

Images/Photos
1. Biblewalks: http://www.biblewalks.com
2. Journey to the Holy Land: http://lluker.faculty.ltss.edu/
3. K. C. Hanson's Home Page: http://www.kchanson.com (look for link to photos)

Links Directories
1. Web Directory of Biblical Studies: http://www.bible-researcher.com/links.html
2. Resource Pages for Biblical Studies: http://torreys.org/bible/
3. Wabash Center: http://www.wabashcenter.wabash.edu/resources/guide_headings.aspx (huge site)
4. Religion Online: http://www.religion-online.org/
5. Gregorian Chant Home Page: http://www.music.princeton.edu/chant_html/

Social Location/Social Analysis
1. K. C. Hanson's Home Page: http://www.kchanson.com
2. Early Christian Writings and Social World: http://www.torreys.org/bible/biblia03.html (up-to-date; regularly modified)
3. Hartford Institute for Religion Research: http://www.hartfordinstitute.org (demographic info for congregational studies and practical theology; downloadable articles)
4. Association of Religion Data Archive: http://www.thearda.com (demographic info about religion in the U.S.)
5. Center for Immigration Studies: http://www.cis.org (nonpartisan U.S. organization on study of immigration policy in the U.S.)
6. U.S. Census: http://www.census.gov

Ministry Websites
1. Ministry articles: http://www.religion-online.org/listbycategory.asp?Cat=54
2. Life Journal www.enewhope.org

3. www.Christianpowerpoints.com
4. www.Digitaljuice.com
5. www.eyeeffectsworship.com
6. www.Ultimatepowerpoint.com

DVD Background for words—www.Worshipfilms.com

Iconography Website—www.aug.edu/augusta/iconography/index.html

Sound Tech Web sites:
www.learnchurchsound.com
The ultimate church sound operator hand book (google)

Multimedia Section—General gear online site:
www.bhphotovideo.com
www.bhproaudio.com
www.sweetwater.com
www.musiciansfriend.com
www.guitarcenter.com

Worship Images compatible w/ MediaShout
Oxygen multimedia
http://www.oxygen-multimedia.com/page/O2/CTGY/DN

Index of Art with the lectionary or Bible characters
http://www.textweek.com/art/art.htm

Other bookmarks I have but don't use frequently
http://www.imagevine.com/index.htm
http://www.worshipgraphics.com/
www.highwayvideo.com

APPENDIX 11

Microphones: Design & Application

Assembled by Josh Park

Microphone: a transducer that changes one form of energy (sound wave) into another corresponding forms of energy (electrical signal).

Microphone placement rule:
1. There are no rules, only guidelines.
2. The overall sound of an audio signal is no better than the weakest link in the signal path.
3. Use "good rule" = good musician + good acoustic + good mike + good placement= GOOD SOUND.
4. USE common sense.

Five types of Microphone:
1. The dynamic microphone: operates by using electromagnetic induction to generate an output signal. Example: SM58

2. The Ribbon microphone: It works on electromagnetic induction, however, it uses a diaphragm of extremely thin aluminum ribbon (2 micrometers).

3. The condenser microphone: This operate on an electrostatic principle rather than the electromagnetic principle that's used by the dynamic & ribbon mics.

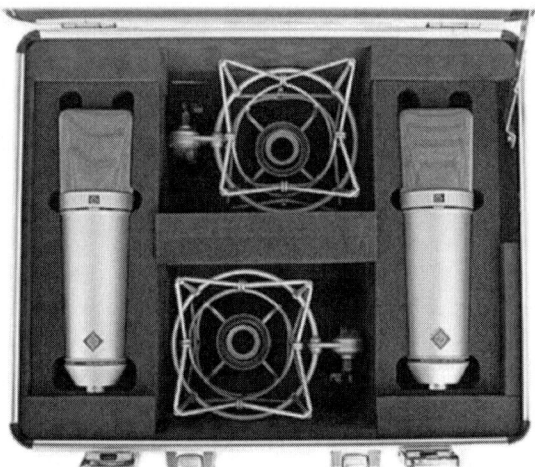

4. The electric-condenser microphone: this works on the same operating principles as an externally polarized condenser, except that a static polarizing charge in permanently stored within the diaphragm or the mic's backplate.
5. PZM: pressure zone microphone (Boundary), Phase coherent cardioid

Microphone Patterns
Directional response: Omni, Bidirectional, Cardioid, hyper-cardioid, super-cardioid, and etc...

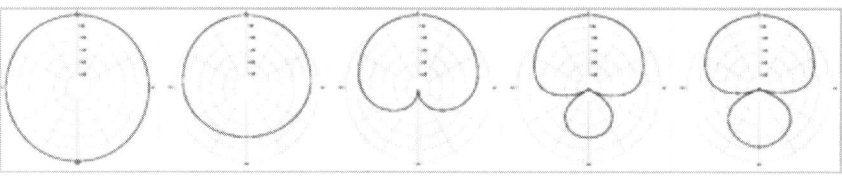

Omni　　　Subcardioid　　　Cardioid　　　Supercardioid　　　Hypercardioid

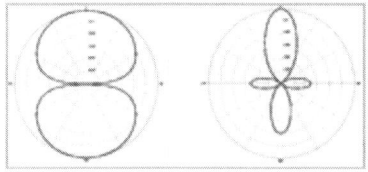

Bidirectional　　Shotgun

Microphone Techniques
1. Distant microphone placement: most preferred for natural tone but be aware of reflections.
2. Close microphone placement (accent mic.): needed in order to gain isolation. Used a lot in live setting.
3. In multiple microphone setup, be aware of 3:1 rule.
4. Stereo Mike technique:
    a. Spaced stereo technique
    b. XY crossed cardioid pair
    c. Blumlein crossed bidirectional pair
    d. M/S stereo pair
    e. Near coincidence pair
    f. Many more...

APPENDIX 12

Projection Software—Overview and Comparison

(Assembled by Drew Walsh)

PROPRESENTER:
Learning Curve: extremely user friendly; easy to learn; video applications are easiest as compared to other projection software

Comparison to Mediashout:
Propresenter: easier to use; software is straightforward so it is harder to make user mistakes; the best for video applications (least amount of glitches); best for moving backgrounds; compatible with Mac; more expensive; Macs in general are more expensive; does not have problems with viruses

Mediashout: can be difficult to navigate; software more complicated so it is easier to make user mistakes; good for video application but has a fair amount of glitches; good for moving backgrounds; compatible with PC; less expensive; PCs in general are more inexpensive; susceptible to virus

Why buy this product? Propresenter is the best projection software on the market. It is especially great for church applications when high quality backgrounds, moving backgrounds, and video will be used.

MEDIASHOUT:
Learning Curve: decently user friendly but you will need to get out the directions for sure; will be much easier to use if you are extremely familiar with PCs; video applications are decently easy to use

Why buy this product? Mediashout is a great product for churches who are currently running their media with PCs and PC based software. It is a cheaper option yet still offers high quality features. Budget wise, this Mediashout will be a church's best option.

KEYNOTE:
Learning Curve: very easy to use; very easy to learn; very clean looking and easy to navigate

Comparison to Powerpoint:
Keynote: easier to navigate; more user friendly; Mac based; comes with iWork; video applications are easy to use but quality is just ok; as far as I know moving backgrounds are not an option

Powerpoint: decently easy to navigate; PC based; been around longer; comes with Microsoft Office; video applications are more difficult to use and not the best quality; as far as I know moving backgrounds are not an option

Why buy this product? If your church is using Macs then this is your cheapest, best option. It is very similar to Powerpoint, but is more user friendly, has less glitches, and is not susceptible to viruses. In addition, you can customize backgrounds and add video. If your computer already has iWork then it is free!

POWERPOINT:
Learning Curve: decently easy to use and learn; harder to navigate; more people are familiar with this program, though, because it has been around for so long

Why buy this product? If your church is using PC computers and based software then this is your cheapest, best option. You can customize backgrounds and add video, though both are a little glitchy. If your computer already has Microsoft Office then it is free!

APPENDIX 13

Music & Worship Budget Considerations

"Fail to plan, plan to fail."

Your yearly budget should be done AFTER your yearly plan is complete (Chapter 17). Most "budget" people are "bean counters" and don't relate to or understand us "Artist" types, so you will have to show and explain the numbers if you want to execute your dreams. The following are some general budgeting categories.

Sheet Music
   Computing a Sheet Music Budget for large ensembles.
      How many times will they perform? Half the time, use new music, half the time reuse music that has been performed before. Only buy Musicals that you can use at least half the songs leading up to the musical.
   For example: A choir who will sing 45 times a year should buy 20 new Anthems, and a Christmas and Easter Cantata from which they can sing 4–5 songs.
   Ensembles—List each ensemble with the number of performances, members, and average cost of a piece of sheet music. Be sure to include any musicals.
   Subscription Series—These publishers send music and recordings to you for a fee.

Leadership Training
   Conferences—Worship or Music Conferences.
   Seminars—More specific to your needs. Always try to take someone along.

Equipment Maintenance
   Piano—Tuned twice per year.
   Electronic Instruments—Budget 15% of the purchase price for repairs.
   Cords—Replace every year or every other year, depending upon usage.
   Mics—Repair and replacement.
   Wardrobe (choir robes cleaning and replacement, etc.)

Equipment Purchase (Capital Expenses)
   Necessities—Always include an explanation of the need for any large purchase.
   Dreams—Maintain a folder or list of stuff you would love to have, in case someone gets the vision to write you a check!

Clinicians & Substitutes
   A Fresh set of Ears—Try to bring someone in once a year to conduct your program. It helps the participants, and it inspires you.
   Vacation Replacement—Who will replace you when on vacation or attending conferences? If you may have to pay someone, budget for it.

Event Planning
    Special Services—Are there Holiday Service expectations? Plan and budget accordingly.
    Concerts—Will you invite outside artists to perform for your Church?

Other Professional Personnel
    Music Librarian, Secretary
    Accompanists—If your accompanist volunteers, fine, but you may get what you pay for. If you pay, do your homework on the requirements for Independent Contractor status.
    Auxiliary Musicians—Whether you hire the same people week after week, or on an occasional basis, be sure to keep good records, and be aware of the Tax requirements.

APPENDIX 14

Ensemble Concepts for Worship Singers & Bands

Worship Singers
    I. Role/Function = Eph. 2 Bricks into a spiritual house
        Get into circle, by roles
        Lead Soprano determines the Phrasing/Style
        Mel/Har/Blaster—1 person only
        Build from top
        Melody
        Harmony
        Blaster

Always have 1 male and 1 female voice on the melody, to let the people know what they should be singing.

    II. Variety of Tone/Sound/Blend—Pick a song, and practice these different styles
        Breathy
        Edgy
        Unison
        Harmony
        Dynamics—3 levels
            Put one in charge of changing

    III. Adjustment = Koininia
        Pick a song; have one singer change style/dynamics, and everyone else adapt
        Styles
            Latin
            Gospel
            Hymn
            Rock
            Ballad

    IV. Leader = Servant
        Make others successful
        Lead the way/get out of the way

Worship Bands
  I. Role/Function = Eph. 2 Bricks into a spiritual house
      Mel/Har/Rhythm = priority in Worship leading
      Build a sound from the bottom
          Bass & Drums
          Rhythm Guitar & Keyboard
          Lead Guitar/Sax
          Singers

  II. Adjustment = Koininia
      Have one player change style, everyone else adapt

  III. Accompaniment = Servant
      Make others successful
      Lead the way/get out of the way
      Dynamics—3 levels
          Put one in charge of changing

  IV. Ability = Sacrifice to God
      Practice
      Styles—Learn
          Gospel—Piano is lead voice
          Latin—Bass & Percussion are lead voice
          Rock—Guitar & Drums are lead voice
          Ballad—Piano is lead voice
      Reading Charts

APPENDIX 15

Personal Monitoring Systems

Assembled by Josh Park and Drew Walsh

Definition: Systems used to determine levels of sound in an occupied area by a person

Two types: a) floor Monitors b) In-ear monitors

In-ear Monitors
So many companies make these products.
Shure, Aviom, Sanhiesser, Nady, Ultimate ears

The best of the best: Ultimate ears www.ultimateears.com
This company makes hi-tech in-ear.
They are made with 3 types of drivers.
  Single driver: mainly designed for vocalists
  Double Driver: For band
  Triple driver: for band-base players
  4 speaker crossover: with subwoofer

Some of their monitors are custom made. They have in-ears designed for rock, country, hip hop music. One can have these monitors custom fit for one's ears.

Great reviews from musicians, music lovers and listeners, from Fox Business News, Forbes.

Shure has great in-ears too with drivers and sound isolation like SCL 3, SCL 4 and SCL 5.

Shure
This company provides all accessories including ear monitors, receiver, and transmixer.

Cheapest—PSM200 It is a sufficient for entry level performers. The Shure P2TRE2-H2 PSM 200 Wireless Personal Monitor System includes P2T TransMixer, P2R Hybrid Receiver, and **E2 Sound Isolating Earphones.** This inexpensive in-ear personal monitor system offers Shure's quality and innovative new features. The receiver is dual-function (wired or wireless) and has a built-in limiter for hearing protection. LED indicators for power, RF signal strength, limiter, and battery level. The transmitter is frequency-agile (8 channels per system), allows up to 4 simultaneous compatible systems, **and has a range of 300' under optimum conditions**. Volume controls let you create your own mix. Earphone is high-fidelity and has interchangeable flex and foam sleeves to give a perfect fit. May be susceptible to interference.

PSM400 is the next one up. This is bigger and better with more options on mixing one's sound.

At its heart is the P4M Personal Monitor Mixer-a 4-channel, 2-bus stereo mic/line mixer designed to optimize in-ear monitoring. It allows easy access to and control over each input source. 2 auxiliary inputs can be used to add channels from other sources. Includes the P4T Wireless Transmitter with audio limiter and removable/combinable antennas, P4R Wireless Bodypack Receiver and **E3 earphones**

Good for bigger church with more complex sound. You can get one with a personal mixer.

PSM 700
The PSM®700 series offers advanced controls and features that make it easy to quickly locate and lock in the clearest frequency, prevent distortion and minimize the number of antennas required to send mixes.

All systems and wireless bodypack receivers are available with either SCL5 or gray SCL3 Sound Isolating Earphones.

PSM®900 Personal Monitor Systems
COMING SOON

The PSM®900 Wireless Personal Monitor System from Shure offers an unprecedented combination of superb audio quality, robust RF performance, and category-leading features for the most demanding professional applications. All new, patent pending CueMode allows the sound engineer to monitor different stage mixes with the touch of a button. Precision front-end RF filtering significantly reduces dropouts from RF interference, and the enhanced digital stereo encoder provides excellent stereo separation and audio clarity.

Remember that you can buy some of these gadgets separately.

Other brand worth mentioning was a pack of 4 in-ears from Galaxy AS-ALS-4 Monitor system.
Seemed decent with a radius of 300 ft.
You can also look at sennheiser.

APPENDIX 16

Evaluating A Worship Service

1. The Plan: What was our service plan; our roadmap? Was it a theological plan? Did the order in which we did things make theological sense? Did we observe the biblical pattern of revelation and response, or the historical plan of Word and Table, or some other well thought out pattern?

2. The Story: Whose story was emphasized? Did we retell and rehearse God's story of creation and resurrection, reconciliation and the coming Kingdom, or did we emphasize the People's stories? Did we celebrate the whole story of God, or just the parts we like? Did we invite and expect our people to insert their individual stories and testimonies into God's grand story; to embed themselves into something much bigger; or did they leave thinking their own story to be primary?

3. The Action: Where was the action happening: on the Platform, or with the People? Presentation, or participation? Are these gathered Believers a Congregation, or an audience?

If we say that we gather for CORPORATE worship, was our service truly corporate? And was it truly service? Did the people do most of the work, or was the real action happening on the platform? Could most of the service have been pulled-off if the congregation had gotten locked out? How much time did the congregation spend doing, as opposed to watching? Did the people engage more than two of their senses as they performed this delightful work of worship?

4. The Result: Did the people recognize and accept the responsibility of their own offering to God, or did they allow it to be done for them? Did people leave commenting on how the people up front did, or asking God how they did? And did they leave with a reminder, or with a mission.

APPENDIX 17

Vocalist Tryouts

	Name	Range	Intonation	Style	Comments
1					
2					
3					
4					
5					
6					
7					
8					
9					
10					

APPENDIX 18

Practical Advice for Worship Leaders

1. To encourage people to participate, try to choose songs most will know. Be careful of using more than one new song in a set, and make sure it is quickly accessible. If you're a visiting leader, do your homework (know, in advance, the songs with which the people are familiar).

2. To enable people to sing with you, it will help to choose accessible keys. What vocally works for you might not work for the people.

3. If you want people to actively listen to you sing, say so, and tell them why.

4. To inspire people to follow you, tell them where you are going. Have a theological plan; don't just choose songs that groove well together.

5. To add some aesthetic interest, try to incorporate a variety of styles in an assortment keys.

6. To help people to engage, provide several avenues of response. Do more than simply "stand and sing."

7. To get people to think as well as to feel, beware of aimless repetition.

8. To invite an authentic response, tell people why you want them to stand, kneel, raise hands, clap, etc. Don't assume, and if you don't know the "why," go figure it out.

9. To lead people to marvel, rejoice, repent or praise, incorporate the Scriptures for guidance. Be inviting, but don't demand that they feel what you feel.

10. To facilitate worship, sprinkle your prayers and transitions with the various attributes of God. Don't just rely upon the song lyrics.

11. If you care more about the people than the platform, design worship for the seats, not the stage.

12. For Holiday services, don't be afraid of traditional music; people expect it.

NOTE: don't start a Christmas or Easter service with a song that less than 90% of the people will know. Unless you have been teaching a specific song in preparation, don't do music newer than five years old at any Holiday service.

APPENDIX 19

Resources from Sound & Light Publishing

iPhone App for Commuter Worship

Daily worship . . . in both print and audio formats.
Read or listen. Your choice. Guided moments of praise and worship.
30 Worship Devotionals.
To Order go to: www.RoadmapsForWorship.com

DVD Teaching Curriculum
To View the Informational Video go to:
http://www.youtube.com/watch?v=MqE_3gVzjhs

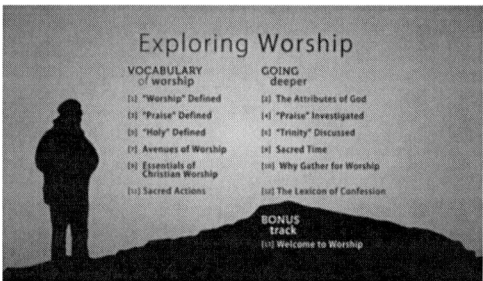

Exploring Worship for Home Groups, Choirs & Worship Teams
- DVD includes 13 brief videos, shot in high-def.
- Extensive Before/After Discussion Questions.
- The videos are presented in pairs, so that the first introduces the concept, while the second delves deeper into that topic.
- Discussion-oriented, 6-week Home Group Series.
- The videos can also be used alone as a short devotional, or a quick and meaty break during Choir or Worship Team rehearsal.

To Order go to: http://roadmapsforworship.com/?page_id=1720

Roadmaps for Daily Worship
100 Daily Devotionals

Devotions born from Scripture and Designed for Worship
God has given a well-lit path into His presence.
All we need to do is to walk the path every day.
With our whole heart, mind, soul, and strength.
To Order go to: http://roadmapsforworship.com/?page_id=1411

Dictionary of Everyday Theology and Culture

A great new **Dictionary** from **NavPress**.

450 Pages of clear definitions of theological terms
(Worship; Justification; Praise; etc.)

Excellent **applications** to real life.
Written by Scholars who use plain English!
To Order go to: http://roadmapsforworship.com/?page_id=1404

Vocal & Instrumental CDs & Downloads

Available on iTunes

To see more music from Sound & Light Music go to:
http://roadmapsforworship.com/?page_id=179

VI

Recommended List Of Books

Adam, Adolf. *The Liturgical Year*. Collegeville, Minnesota: The Liturgical Press, 1981.

Advisory Board of the Conversion to Judaism Resource Center. *Baptism—Jewish; Immersion Conversion to Judaism* Resource Center. Database online. Available from http://www.convert.org/process.htm. Accessed 8 September 2006.

Allen, Ronald B. *Lord of Song*. Portland, Oregon: Multnomah Press, 1985.

———. *Praise! A Matter of Life and Breath*. Nashville: Thomas Nelson.1978.

———. *The Wonder of Worship*. Nashville: Thomas Nelson, 2001.

Barna, George, et al. *Experience God in Worship*. Loveland, Colorado: Group Publishing, 2000.

Bass, Dorothy, C. *Receiving The Day*. San Francisco: Josey-Bass, 2000.

Bateman, Herbert W. IV (Gen. Ed.). *Authentic Worship: Hearing Scripture's Voice, Applying Its Truths*. Grand Rapids, Michigan: Kregel Inc., 2002.

Best, Ernest *1 Peter* in *New Century Bible*. Grand Rapids: Eerdmans, 1971.

Best, Harold M. *Music Through The Eyes Of Faith*. San Francisco: HarperCollins Publishers, 1993.

———. *Unceasing Worship: Biblical Perspectives on Worship and the Arts*. Downers Grove, Illinois: InterVarsity Press, 2003.

Bonhoeffer, Deitrich. *Life Together*. New York, New York: Harper & Row Publishers, 1954.

———. *Psalms: The Prayer Book of the Bible*. Minneapolis: Augsburg, 1970.

Borchert, Gerald L. *Responding to Mystery: A Worship Introduction to the New Testament*. Chalice Press, 2006.

Bradshaw, Paul. *Early Christian Worship*. Collegeville, Minnesota: The Liturgical Press, 1996.

Bridge, Donald and David Phypers. *The Water That Divides: A Survey of the Doctrine of Baptism*. Downers Grove, Illinois: Christian Focus Publications, 1998.

Byars, Ronald P. *Christian Worship: Glorifying and Enjoying God*. Louisville: Geneva Press, 2000.

Carson, D.A., ed., *Worship By The Book*. Grand Rapids, Michigan: Zondervan, 2002.

Clifton, Donald O. and Edward "Chip" Anderson. *StrengthsQuest*. Washington, D.C.: The Gallup Organization, 2003.

Clinton, Robert J. *The Making of a Leader*. Colorado Springs, Colorado: NavPress, 1988.

Cross, Anthony and Philip Thompson, ed. *Baptist Sacramentalism*. Waynesboro, Georgia: Paternoster, 2003.

Davis, Ken. Secrets of *Dynamic Communication*. Grand Rapids, Michigan: Zondervan Publishing House, 1991.

Dawn, Marva J. *A Royal Waste of Time*. Grand Rapids, Michigan: Eerdmans Publishing Company, 1999.

———. *Reaching Out without Dumbing Down*. Grand Rapids, Michigan: Eerdmans Publishing Company, 1995.

———. *The Sense of Call: A Sabbath Way of Life for Those who Serve God, the Church, and the World*. Grand Rapids: Eerdmans, 2006.

Dawn, Marva and Eugene Peterson. *The Unnecessary Pastor: Rediscovering the Call*. Grand Rapids: Eerdmans, 1999.

DePree, Max. *Leadership is an Art*. New York, New York: Bantam Doubleday Publishing Group, Inc., 1989.

Fast, Julius. *Body Language*. New York, New York: Pocket Books, 1970.

———. *Worship in Spirit and Truth*. Phillipsburg, New Jersey: P&R Publishing, 1996.

Frankforter, A. Daniel. *Stones For Bread: A Critique of Contemporary Worship*. Louisville, Kentucky: John Knox Press, 2001.

Garland, David E. *Colossians and Philemon in NIV Application Commentary*. Grand Rapids: Zondervan, 1998.

Gibbs, Alfred P. *Worship: The Christian's Highest Occupation*. Kansas City, Kansas: Walterick Publishers, (no date given).

Grenz, Stanley J. *Theology for the Community of God*. Grand Rapids, Michigan: Eerdmans Publishing Company, 1994.

Hackett, Charles D. & Don E. Saliers. *The Lord Be With You*. Cleveland, Ohio: OSL Publications, 1990.

Hammett, John S. *Biblical foundations for Baptist Churches: A Contemporary Ecclesiology*. Grand Rapids, Michigan: Kregel, 2005.

Hickman, Saliers, Stookey, White. *The New Handbook of the Christian Year*. Nashville, Tennessee: Abingdon Press, 1992.

Hill, Andrew E. *Enter His Courts With Praise: Old Testament Worship for the New Testament Church*. Grand Rapids, Michigan: Baker Book House, 1996.

Horton, Michael. *In the Face of God: The Dangers & Delights of Spiritual Intimacy*. Dallas, Texas: Word Publishing, 1996.

Howard, Thomas. *Evangelical Is Not Enough: Worship Of God In Liturgy And Sacrament*. San Francisco, California: Ignatius Press, 1984.

Hustad, Donald P. *True Worship*. Carol Stream, Illinois: Hope Publishing Co., 1998.

———. *Jubilate II: Church Music in Worship and Renewal*. Carol Stream, Illinois: Hope Publishing Co., 1993.

Johnson, Maxwell E. *Between Memory and Hope, Readings on the Liturgical Year*. Collegeville, Minnesota: The Liturgical Press, 2000.

Johnson, Todd E. (ed.) *The Conviction of Things Not Seen: Worship and Ministry in the 21st Century*. Grand Rapids, Michigan: Brazos Press, 2002.

Kidd, Reggie M. *With One Voice*. Grand Rapids, Michigan: Baker Books, 2005.

Kidner, Derek. *Psalms 1–72, Tyndale Old Testament Commentaries*. Downers Grove, Illinois, InterVarsity Press, 1978.

Lathrop, Gordon. *What Are the Essentials of Christian Worship?*. Minneapolis: Augsburg Fortress, 1994.

Leonard, Janice E., "The Covenant Basis of Biblical Worship." In *Biblical Foundations of Christian Worship,* ed. Robert E. Webber, 56. Vol 1, *The Complete Library of Christian Worship*. Peabody, Massachusetts: Hendrickson Publishers, Inc., 1993.

Lewis, C.S. *Reflections on the Psalms*. San Diego: Harcourt Brace Jovanovich, 1958.

———. *The Weight of Glory & Other Addresses*. San Francisco: Eerdmans, 1965 (orig., 1949).

Liesch, Barry. *The New Worship: Straight Talk on Music and the Church*. Grand Rapids: Baker Books, 1996.

Malefyt, Norma deWaal & Howard Vanderwell. *Designing Worship Together: Models and Strategies for Worship Planning*. Herndon, Virginia: The Alban Institute, 2005.

Martin, Ralph P. *Colossians: The Church's Lord and the Christian's Liberty*. Grand Rapids: Zondervan, 1972.

———. *The New Century Bible Commentary: Colossians and Philemon*. Grand Rapids: Eerdmans, 1971.

———. *Worship In The Early Church*. Grand Rapids: Wm. B. Eerdmans Publishing Co., 1964.

McKnight, Scott. *1 Peter* in *NIV Application Commentary*. Grand Rapids: Zondervan, 1996.

Miller, Rex. *The Millennium Matrix: Reclaiming the Past, Reframing the Future of the Church*. San Francisco, California: Jossey-Bass, 2004.

Mitman, Russell F. *Worship in the Shape of Scripture*. Cleveland: Pilgrim Press, 2001.

Moseley, Ron. *The Jewish Background of Christian Baptism*. Sherwood, Arkansas: Arkansas Institute of Holy Land Studies, 2002. Database online. Available from http://www.Haydid.org.html. Accessed 8 September 2006.

Navarro, Kevin. *The Complete Worship Leader*. Grand Rapids, Michigan: Baker Books, 2001.

O'Toole. *Leading Change*. New York, New York: Ballantine Books, 1996.

Old, Hughes Oliphant. *Leading In Prayer*. Grand Rapids: Wm. B. Eerdmans Publishing Co., 1995.

Owens, Ron. *Return to Worship*. Nashville, Tennessee: Broadman & Holdman Publishers, 1999.

Peterson, David. *Engaging with God: A Biblical Theology of Worship*. Downers Grove, Illinois: InterVarsity Press, 1992.

Pfatteicher, Philip H. *Liturgical Spirituality*. Valley Forge, Pennsylvania: Trinity Press, 1997.

Plantinga, Cornelius, Jr. & Sue Rozeboom. *Discerning the Spirits: A Guide to Thinking about Christian Worship Today*. Grand Rapids, Michigan: Eerdmans Publishing Co., 2003.

Saliers, Don E. *Worship As Theology*. Nashville: Abingdon Press, 1994.

Schmemann, Alexander. *For the Life of the World: Sacraments and Orthodoxy*. Crestwood, New York: St. Vladimir's Seminary Press, 1973.

———. *Of Water and the Spirit: A Liturgical Study of Baptism*. Crestwood, New York: St. Vladimir's Seminary Press, 1974.

———. *The Eucharist: Sacrament of the Kingdom*. Crestwood, New York: St. Vladimir's Seminary Press, 1987.

Siewert, Alison, ed. *Worship Team Handbook*. Downers Grove, Illinois: InterVarsity Press, 1998.

Snodgrass, Klyne. *Ephesians* in *The NIV Application Commentary*. Grand Rapids: Zondervan, 1996.

Snyder, James L., comp. *Tozer on Worship and Entertainment*. Camp Hill Pennsylvania: Wing Spread Publishers, 1997.

Stone, Howard W. & James O. Duke, *How To Think Theologically*. Minneapolis: Fortress Press, 2006.

Stookey, Laurence Hull. Calendar, *Christ's Time for the Church*. Nashville, Tennessee: Abingdon Press, 1996.

Talley, Thomas J. *The Origins of the Liturgical Year*. Collegeville, Minnesota: The Liturgical Press, 1991.

The Holy Bible: New International Version. New York International Bible Society.

Torrance, James B. *Worship, Community and the Triune God of Grace*. Downers Grove, Illinois: InterVarsity Press, 1996.

Tozer, A.W. *The Attributes of God, vol. 2*. Camp Hill: Christian Publications, Inc. 2001.

———. *The Knowledge of The Holy*. San Francisco: Harper & Row, 1961.

———. *The Pursuit of God*. Camp Hill: Christian Publications, Inc. 1982.

———. *Whatever Happened to Worship?*, comp. Gerald B. Smith. Camp Hill Pennsylvania: Wing Spread Publishers, 1985.

Underhill, Evelyn. *Worship*. Guildford, Surrey, UK: Eagle, 1936, revised 1991.

VanderZee, Leonard J. *Christ, Baptism and the Lord's Supper*. Downers Grove, Illinois: IVP, 2004.

Vogel, Dwight W. editor. *Primary Sources of Liturgical Theology*. Collegeville, Minnesota: The Liturgical Press, 2000.

Webber, Robert E., ed. *The Complete Library of Christian Worship, 7 vols*. Peabody, Massachusetts: Hendrickson Publishers, Inc., 1993.

———. *Ancient-Future Worship: Proclaiming and Enacting God's Narrative*. Grand Rapids, Michigan: Baker Books., 2008.

———. *People of the Truth*. Eugene, Oregon: Wipf and Stock Publishers, 2001.

———. *Rediscovering the Christian Feasts*. Peabody, Massachusetts: Hendrickson Publishers, Inc., 2001.

———. *Worship Is A Verb*. Peabody, Massachusetts: Hendrickson Publishers, 1992.

Webb-Mitchell, Brett P. *Christly Gestures*. Grand Rapids, Michigan: Eerdmans Publishing, 2003.

Welker, Michael. *What Happens in Holy Communion?*. Grand Rapids, Michigan: Eerdmans, 2000.

Westermann, Claus. *The Living Psalms*. Edinburgh: T. & T. Clark, Ltd., 1989.

———. *The Praise of God in the Psalms,* trans. Keith R. Crim. Richmond, Virginia: John Knox, 1965.

White, James F. *A Brief History of Christian Worship*. Nashville: Abingdon Press, 1993.

———. *Christian Worship in North America*. Collegeville, Minnesota: The Liturgical Press, 1997.

———. *Documents of Christian Worship*. Louisville: Westminster John Knox Press, 1992.

———. *Introduction To Christian Worship*. Collegeville, Minnesota: The Liturgical Press, 1980.

Wiersbe, Warren W. *Real Worship*. Grand Rapids, Michigan: Baker Books, 2000.

Wilde, James A. *At That Time, Cycles and Seasons in the Life of a Christian*. Chicago: Liturgy Training Publications, 1989.

Witvliet, John D. *Worship Seeking Understanding: Windows into Christian Practice*. Grand Rapids, Michigan: Baker Books, 2003.

Wren, Brian. *Praying Twice: The Music and Words of Congregational Song*. Louisville: Westminster John Knox Press, 2000.

Wyrtzen, Don. *A Musician Looks at the Psalms*? Grand Rapids, Michigan: Day Break Books, 1988.